S0-BCX-814

# Start Your Own Medical Practice

## A Guide to All the Things They Don't Teach You in Medical School about Starting Your Own Practice

by Judge William Huss
and Marlene M. Coleman, MD

SPHINX® PUBLISHING
AN IMPRINT OF SOURCEBOOKS, INC.®
NAPERVILLE, ILLINOIS
www.SphinxLegal.com

Copyright © 2006 by William Huss and Marlene M. Coleman
Cover and internal design © 2006 by Sourcebooks, Inc.®
Cover art © 2006 by Punchstock

All rights reserved. No part of this book may be reproduced in any form or by any electronic or
mechanical means including information storage and retrieval systems—except in the case of brief
quotations embodied in critical articles or reviews—without permission in writing from its publisher, Sourcebooks, Inc.® Purchasers of the book are granted a license to use the forms contained
herein for their own personal use. No claim of copyright is made in any government form reproduced herein. Sourcebooks and the colophon are registered trademarks of Sourcebooks, Inc.

First Edition: 2006

Published by: **Sphinx® Publishing, An Imprint of Sourcebooks, Inc.®**

Naperville Office
P.O. Box 4410
Naperville, Illinois 60567-4410
630-961-3900
Fax: 630-961-2168
www.sourcebooks.com
www.SphinxLegal.com

This publication is designed to provide accurate and authoritative information in regard to the
subject matter covered. It is sold with the understanding that the publisher is not engaged in rendering legal, accounting, or other professional service. If legal advice or other expert assistance is
required, the services of a competent professional person should be sought.
*From a Declaration of Principles Jointly Adopted by a Committee of the*
*American Bar Association and a Committee of Publishers and Associations*

### This product is not a substitute for legal advice.
*Disclaimer required by Texas statutes*

### This product is not a substitute for medical advice.

## Library of Congress Cataloging-in-Publication Data

Huss, William H.
  Start your own medical practice : a guide to all the things they don't
teach you in medical school about starting your own practice / by William
Huss and Marlene M. Coleman. -- 1st ed.
     p. ; cm.
  Includes index.
  ISBN-13: 978-1-57248-574-7 (pbk. : alk. paper)
  ISBN-10: 1-57248-574-4 (pbk. : alk. paper)
  1. Medicine--Practice. 2. Medical offices. 3. Health
facilities--Business management. I. Coleman, Marlene. II. Title.
  [DNLM: 1. Practice Management, Medical--organization &
administration--United States. 2. Practice Management, Medical--legislation
& jurisprudence--United States. W 80 H972s 2006]
  R728.H86 2006
  610--dc22
                                                          2006030260

Printed and bound in the United States of America.
SB — 10  9  8  7  6  5  4  3  2

*Dedicated to you, the physician
devoted to creating something
that has never existed before—
your medical practice.*

# Acknowledgments

Volumes have been written on each subject in this book, and we owe a great debt to the many people who gave us encouragement and support—especially our families, friends, colleagues, and students. The authors we studied for this book have our deepest gratitude.

We are especially grateful to the many people at the Cooperative of American Physicians—Mutual Protective Trust (CAP—MPT), whose expertise and assistance have been invaluable. Dr. Coleman's colleagues and special faculty at USC Keck School of Medicine, especially in the ICM program, are awesome in their teaching professionalism and their concern for the importance of a balanced life for physicians.

Michael Bowen, Managing Editor at Sphinx Publishing, is the inspiration for the ideas in this book. We are honored that he asked us to write it and helped us understand the vision and organization for it. His talent is invaluable. Lisa Findley's ability and diligence in editing has helped our book become a reality.

The vital editing and organizing of the materials, without which there would be no book, was the result of the untiring efforts of a real genius, Judy Kleinberg—an author herself. Her spirit and talents can be found throughout the pages of this book.

Both of us are truly honored and thankful for the opportunity to collaborate on this project. We hope that the wisdom that is shared in these pages will inform and enliven your practice and guide you toward professional success and fulfillment.

# Contents

*Preface* . . . . . . . . . . . . . . . . . . . . . . . . . . . . . . *xiii*

## I. SETTING UP YOUR MEDICAL PRACTICE

*Chapter 1: Finding the Right Location* . . . . . . . . . *1*
    Locating Your Practice
    Office Space
    Negotiating the Lease

*Chapter 2: Creating Your Practice* . . . . . . . . . . . *9*
    Writing a Business Plan
    New Options in Medicine
    Structuring Your Practice
    Sole Practitioners
    Partnerships
    Limited Liability Partnerships
    Corporations
    LLC or Subchapter S Corporations
    Firm Agreements

## Chapter 3: Business Formation Fundamentals . . 27
Important Preliminaries

## Chapter 4: Office Design, Layout, and Furnishings . . . . . . . . . . . . . . . . . . . . . 31
Work Space Planning
*Doctor's Office Checklist*
The Waiting Room
*Basic Waiting Area Checklist*
Support Staff Area
Common Spaces
*Employee Lounge Checklist*
Filing Systems
Décor
Maintaining the Office

## Chapter 5: Equipment . . . . . . . . . . . . . . . . . 41
To Buy, Lease, or Rent
*Basic Office Equipment Checklist*
*Examination Room and Lab Supplies Checklist*
*Office Supplies Checklist*
*Supply Inventory Form*
Telephones
*Communications Checklist*
*Telephone Intake Form*
*Telephone Log Sheet*
Gearing Up: Computer Hardware and Software
Day-to-Day Operations
Electronic Health Records
*Computer Discussion and Planning Checklist*

## Chapter 6: Personnel . . . . . . . . . . . . . . . . . 65
Civil Rights
Work Safety and Fairness
Medical Office Personnel

Who to Hire
The Interview
Policies and Procedures
*Policy Manual Checklist*
*Procedures Manual Checklist*


## Chapter 7: Outside Support Services . . . . . . . . . 79
Finding Trustworthy Consultants
Business Managers
Accountants
Banks
Insurance
*Insurance Checklist*


## Chapter 8: Your Medical Library . . . . . . . . . . . . 89
Getting Books
The Electronic Medical Library
Essential Medical Library Starters
*Medical Library Checklist*


## Chapter 9: Financing . . . . . . . . . . . . . . . . . . . . 93
Raising Capital
Debt Management
Budget
Cash Flow

# II. MANAGING YOUR MEDICAL PRACTICE

## Chapter 10: The Organized Office . . . . . . . . . . 103
Indexing
Setting Up the Charts and Files
Office Management Forms

*Sample Symptom Diary*
*Patient Transfer Form*
*Missed Appointment Notice*
*Referral Acknowledgment*
Administration

## Chapter 11: Fees, Billing, and Collections . . . . 121
Establishing a Fee Structure
In-House Billing
Outsource Billing
Overdue Payments
Delinquent Accounts
*Unpaid Bill Letter*
Skippers
Collection Agencies

## Chapter 12: Ethics . . . . . . . . . . . . . . . . . . . . 131
Ethical Rules
Ethics and Personnel
Unauthorized Practice of Medicine
Doctor Relations with the Public
Sex in the Workplace
Doctor/Patient Fee Disputes
Conflicts of Interest
Terminating a Patient
*Patient Termination Letter*

## Chapter 13: Marketing Your Practice . . . . . . . . 145
Building a Base
Advertising
Keeping Patients

# III. PERSONAL CONSIDERATIONS

## Chapter 14: Medical-Legal Issues . . . . . . . . . . 155
The Physician/Patient Relationship
Physician/Patient Communications and Privileges
The Patient's Privacy Rights
HIPAA
Informed Consent
Advance Directives
The Physician as Witness
Professional Liability
*Anatomy of a Professional Liability Trial Chart*
Anatomy of a Professional Liability Trial
Mediation
Arbitration
ADR Training for Physicians

## Chapter 15: Preventing Malpractice Suits . . . . . 191
Confronting the Unexpected Outcome
The Healing Value of "I'm Sorry"
Clear Communications for Healthy Outcomes
Managing Risk and Reducing Liability
*Checklist for Developing a Risk Management Policy*
Additional Suggestions for Risk Management
*Patient Satisfaction Questionnaire*
*Checklist for Conducting Meetings*
Medical Board Comments for Physicians
Avoiding Common Medical Practice Mistakes

## Chapter 16: Prescription for the Doctor . . . . . . 217
Diagnosing the Doctor
The Stressed Physician
Burnout Assessment and Reduction
Spirituality
Healing…and Staying Healthy

**Chapter 17: A Perspective from Experience. . . . 231**
  Closing Comments

**Appendix: Resources . . . . . . . . . . . . . . . . . 235**

**Index . . . . . . . . . . . . . . . . . . . . . . . . . . . 249**

**About the Authors . . . . . . . . . . . . . . . . . . 257**

# Preface

There are many different ways of launching your medical career. Setting up a doctor's office is just one of them. Some of the other ways are touched upon in this book for comparative purposes, but the focus here is on the unique challenges of beginning your own practice.

Whether you are opening a solo practice right after medical school or going off on your own after years of working in a hospital or group practice, the information in this book helps smooth out the bumps in the road to success. If you are joining others to set up a brand-new office, it helps make your goals more attainable.

Our hope is that this book reduces some of the practical stresses of setting up your business so that you can focus on the aspects of medicine that made you choose the profession in the first place. You have chosen a profession and worked hard to enter it. We want to honor your choice and your work with a sensible, sophisticated guide that directs you to those who can help and provides suggestions so you can help yourself.

We have also compiled the helpful checklists and forms from this book and placed them on the Web for your convenience. Visit **www.sphinxlegal.com/extras/medicalpractice** and download these useful tools for use in your own practice.

chapter one:
# Finding the Right Location

Regardless of its size, your medical practice is not only a business, but also a profession. Businesses need environments and procedures that are geared for productivity and profitability. The things you do at the start of your practice, as well as how you continue to conduct yourself and your business, will have a direct impact on your success.

There is no absolute model for the structure of your practice. Within some general guidelines, it can be adapted to many variables—the number of doctors, their needs, their geographical location, their finances, and all the other factors that are involved in beginning a medical practice. Each situation takes a lot of planning and creative thinking.

One of the first things you will need to consider in setting up your own practice is where to locate it. You need to select a location that is accessible to your patients, allows you to establish and expand your services over the next few years, meets your budget, and satisfies you personally. Your new practice needs a home.

## LOCATING YOUR PRACTICE

The location of your office must be chosen with great care, while keeping your future in mind. Under most circumstances, the time you will spend at that location is going to be considerable—maybe your entire career.

Selecting the location for your office is dependent on many factors. Your choice may be influenced by access to transportation, such as bus lines, subways, parking access, and other factors that make it convenient to patients and staff. Proximity to a hospital may be important if you are planning on having a surgical practice. Personal preferences are also a consideration. You must examine all the factors that are important to you and to the success of your practice based on the needs of your patients.

The location of your medical practice is important, not only because it is very expensive to have to relocate a short time after you open, but also because you begin to build goodwill with the location—your patients know where you are and how to get to you. Your patients develop a feeling of security if they know that you are stable and easy to locate.

Before deciding on a specific location, you may need to decide in what type of community you wish to set up your practice. The size of your community—very small town, a medium-sized city, or a large metropolitan area—can influence the location of your new practice.

Of all the major professions, the practice of medicine provides the most opportunity for specialization. Not only are there increasing numbers of specialties, but there are also subspecialties (and even sub-subspecialties) within them. As you are determining the location of your practice, you will also need to consider how your specialty or subspecialty will relate to community needs and resources.

## Small Towns

In a small town, the cost of rent may be lower than in other areas, and clerical help may be available at lower salaries as well. Standard fees may also be lower. Networking within a small community will probably be easy for someone who is from an established local family, went to school there, and has a network of relatives and friends as a source of patients. Someone who is entering the community cold may initially find it challenging to be accepted as a member of the community. Because residents have fewer options for medical care, doctors who locate in small towns tend to be generalists, even if they hoped to build a specialty practice.

The advantages of opening a practice in a small town include a more personally satisfying lifestyle, potentially lower start-up costs, and access to smaller and more closely-knit networking opportunities for the acquisition of patients. If a large university is located in a small town, its associated medical facilities and teaching hospital will serve a large area, opening opportunities for subspecialties to be practiced in a small town.

The disadvantages of small town practice are isolation from the larger community and distance from hospitals, laboratories, libraries, and specialists. Small towns are less likely to have large office buildings, shared office suites, and other ways of establishing a practice more common in cities.

## Medium-sized Cities

Beginning a practice in a medium-sized city can be quite satisfying because it has the advantages of both a small town and a metropolitan area. It may be close to hospitals and specialists, but may also offer local family and acquaintance networking for patient development. There is often a supply of trained office workers and other services, such as laboratories and treatment facilities.

One of the most favorable characteristics of a medium-sized city for a doctor is the availability of more and larger clubs and organizations that support the networking and referrals necessary to sustain a practice. For example, a medium-sized city can support more than one golf club and other facilities that many doctors use to socialize. As in a small town, a doctor in a medium-sized city has an opportunity to establish a reputation and stand out in the community, becoming well-known relatively quickly, and thereby developing a patient base more easily than in a metropolitan area.

The disadvantages of beginning a practice in a medium-sized city are similar to those of a small town. For instance, there may not be a hospital or a medical library nearby. As in a small town, there may be fewer choices of office buildings, particularly office suites that can be shared.

## *Metropolitan Area*

The advantages of a large city include the proximity to hospitals, labs, and specialists; large and easily accessible medical libraries; and a broad source of patients. With a much larger population to draw from, a city doctor has a greater opportunity to develop a strong specialty practice.

Generally speaking, large metropolitan areas provide the most practical environment for medical specialties and subspecialties because of the larger population base and the institutions providing medical facilities. Laboratories and institutes provide the technical base from which the practitioner can obtain results of tests and other procedures to aid in the diagnosis and treatment of illness. Many of the top medical practitioners of complicated and highly technical surgeries are located in large metropolitan areas, where there may be numerous other resources to support a physician's specialty.

It may be difficult to determine the competition for the kind of practice that you want to begin, although a close examination of the telephone books is a good place to start. The number of doctors may be so large that you will have to join local medical specialty associations in order to get some idea of who the practitioners are in that area.

In large metropolitan areas, wages are higher and expenses are higher, including rent, insurance, and professional services (such as accountants, insurance brokers, bookkeepers, and other specialties). Consequently, the cash flow in a practice located in a large metropolitan area has to be substantially higher than in a small or even medium-sized town.

## OFFICE SPACE

Once you have chosen the general location of your practice, decide what kind of space you will need based upon your financial ability and your personal choices. Your decisions must also include whether you plan to share your practice with one or more other doctors, and whether you will need room to expand.

Office space is one of the most important considerations as you begin your medical practice. Your office constitutes a major expense and also projects the image of who you are and what your practice is all about. Not only are these things important, but you and your staff will be working long hours nearly every day of the week in this space. The atmosphere and comfort of the space will directly affect your psychological and physical well-being.

While shopping for office space, look carefully at the area where you want to practice. Consider the proximity to hospitals, clinics, and other medical offices—all of which may make a location more or less convenient for you and your patients.

Ask about going rates to get an idea of what you may have to spend to be in a particular area. Once you decide that you want to pay a certain amount per square foot of office space and you want a certain number of square feet, then you have an idea of how much it is going to cost. Ask doctors in the area for a referral to a commercial real estate broker experienced in working with medical office space. The broker can assist you with the latest information on rental rates and available amenities, as well as with contract negotiations. Armed with your square foot requirement and your per-square-foot cost, your broker should be able to locate a space within the area you have chosen.

For example, if your per-square-foot budget is somewhat low for that area, a broker may be able to work out a deal whereby you pay the going higher per-square-foot rate but you get a certain number of free parking spaces. In some large cities the parking costs are very high. This can be an important consideration when you find the net cost of renting an office without parking spaces and add the cost of renting parking spaces somewhere else.

If this is your first experience with a commercial lease or if you are unfamiliar with the geographical area, discuss with your broker all of the important aspects of leasing. For example, rents may be very stable, going up, or coming down. Discuss comparable facilities and their annual rates. Specifically, discuss the following topics with your broker:

- the length of the lease, determined by whether rents are increasing or decreasing;
- the cost per square foot;
- additional considerations, such as parking (including access to wheelchair accessible spaces) or parking validations provided by the lessor as a part of the lease;
- the amount of the security deposit;
- the first and last months' rent deposit requirements;
- provisions for maintenance and repairs; and,
- the calculation of *pass-throughs*, taxes, security costs, and so on.

Ask your broker to explain the details concerning your lease. Be sure you understand the subtleties of the document. You may wish to have your attorney review the lease before you sign it.

## NEGOTIATING THE LEASE

Each of the foregoing considerations must be included in the negotiations for the terms of the lease. If you are in a position to bargain, such as during a buyer's market, then press hard for lower per-square-foot costs, more complimentary parking spaces or validations, and lower security deposits. You may be able to negotiate whether the last month's rent is in the full amount or a partial figure.

Think seriously about whether you plan to expand your medical practice to include other doctors. If you are going to expand, then you should include in your negotiations for the lease the option to lease additional space at the rate you are paying at the time you exercise the option. You may even want to include the right of first refusal to a certain number of square feet that are contiguous to your space, if that area becomes available.

# chapter two:
# Creating Your Practice

As you think about setting up your practice, you will feel that you have to do everything at once. The urgency of locating and equipping a space, hiring staff, finding patients, getting a business license, beginning some cash flow, paying off your loans, and scores of other responsibilities will press in on you. There are, in fact, many parallel processes involved in starting your practice. However, your practice begins as an idea, and before you can act on the idea, you have to define it, describe it, and put it in writing. You have to create a business plan.

## WRITING A BUSINESS PLAN

Whether you plan to practice medicine on your own, with another physician, or in a large, multi-doctor office, whatever your specialty and wherever you locate, the road map for reaching your goal lies in a well-executed business plan. Your business plan will not only help you steer your practice's development and keep it on track, but it will also assist you when you are seeking credit, applying for financing, taking on new doctors, and managing your public image.

Most of the decisions you have to make in starting a practice will end up costing you money, so it makes sense to look at the pros and cons of each option. If you make wise and well-informed decisions, you will not have to waste time later undoing problems you could have avoided. The process of creating your business plan will help you know which decisions you have to make as you move toward your goal. When you begin, the plan will have a lot of questions and blank spaces, but by the time you have filled in some of the blanks, you will have created something more than an idea: you will have a medical practice.

Your business plan defines the nature of your business, your customers (patients), your resources, your competition, your short- and long-term financial projections, and your marketing. It should be built on specific and realistic terms—measurable objectives, identified responsibilities and deadlines, and practical budgets. Avoid hype, jargon, superlatives, and uncontrolled optimism. Work toward a plan that is straightforward and simple, so it is easy to implement and easy to update as your business grows.

There are numerous books on how to write a business plan. You may also want to consider using one of the software programs that will guide you step-by-step through the development of your plan, such as the following.

**BizPlanBuilder from Jian**
www.jian.com

**Business Plan Pro from Palo Alto Software**
www.paloalto.com

**PlanMagic Business from Plan Magic Corporation**
http://planmagic.com

**PlanWrite from Business Resource Software, Inc.**
www.brs-inc.com

In addition, you can find free, downloadable business plan templates at **www.score.org/template_gallery.html**, provided in various formats by the nonprofit SCORE (a resource partner of the Small Business Administration), and at **www.bplans.com**, a website devoted to business planning resources.

However you approach the process, you will find that business plans have standard components. While this book cannot provide all of the details you will need to write a business plan, the following list gives a general idea of the sections and scope of a typical plan.

- **Cover sheet:** identifies your practice's name, the date, and your contact information.
- **Table of contents**
- **Executive summary:** a single page that describes in brief and simple terms the highlights of your plan—the who, how, when, what, where, and why of your business.
- **Overview:** describes your practice in more detailed terms, including type of medicine, patients, location and physical plant, business structure, goals, general marketing approach, competition, strengths and weaknesses in the marketplace, operating procedures, staff, insurance, and financial overview. Some of these topics are developed in further detail in the sections that follow.
- **In-depth financial plan:** provides very specific and detailed information on business capitalization, including loans, credit resources, equipment, personnel, office improvement costs, deposits, and other start-up costs; balance sheets, with assets and liabilities; breakeven analyses; profit and loss statements; cash flow, including assumptions; write-offs; draws on income; and, accounting systems. Also provides a three-year operating budget, including a detailed first-year analysis, with all rents, salaries, insurance, loans, taxes, marketing, etc., and

quarterly budgets for the second and third years. Includes supporting documents, such as copies of leases, licenses, partners' personal résumés, tax returns and financial statements, and other relevant documentation.

- **In-depth management plan:** describes in very specific terms what skills you bring to the business in addition to your knowledge of medicine, and how you will manage and use staff to complement those skills and get the work done. Expands upon the information in your résumé, including your management experience, and identifies all staff tasks, responsibilities, resources, costs, benefits, and reporting and decision-making structures.

- **In-depth marketing plan:** details who your patients are and how you will attract them, including all marketing/ advertising strategies and associated budgets, sample materials, measurable goals and system for review, competition information, and specifics on how you will establish your pricing.

You might think that you cannot write a business plan before you have a business, but you may be surprised at how many ideas you have once you start writing them down. These are the ideas that will help you create the practice you really want. As you begin to gather your thoughts and the necessary data, you may discover that your goals are unrealistic—or more easily within reach than you had anticipated.

It takes time to put together an effective business plan, so do not wait until your banker or future partner asks you for one. Take the time now to create a well-reasoned business plan to serve as an action plan that sets out your priorities—a checklist that will continue to guide your business's growth even when you are successfully preoccupied with the practice of medicine.

The information in the chapters that follow will help you fill in the blanks and create the plan that will be the foundation of your business.

# NEW OPTIONS IN MEDICINE

While you may feel quite certain that you will be hanging out your shingle and opening a general or specialist practice, you should also be aware that there are new options available in the practice of medicine. These are ways of structuring a practice that did not exist twenty years ago, and they may offer some physicians better quality of life with more balance and more time for personal pursuits. In particular, practicing concierge medicine; being a hospitalist or intensivist; practicing academic or corporate medicine—any of these arenas may be viable choices for today's physician.

## *Concierge Medicine*

*Concierge*, or boutique, medicine reduces the doctor's patient load and establishes a fee-based enrollment for patients. As an example, a practice might be limited to approximately six hundred patients. The patient pays a retainer—typically $1,500 per year for an individual or $4,000 for a family. For this retainer, the patient receives:

- a comprehensive annual physical exam, which may include lab work-ups, chest X-rays, and EKGs;
- same-day or next-day extended appointments;
- follow-up appointments within twenty-four hours of patient's request;
- recommendations for a nutritionist, fitness trainer, or chiropractor;
- information and follow-up on tertiary care;
- house calls as needed;

- phoned results and recommendations after a lab test or special appointment; and,
- special access phone numbers.

With this annual retainer, doctors become available to the patient twenty-four hours a day, seven days a week. They have fewer patients and are happier being able to give more personalized, quality care to their patients. Also, the patients are happier not having to struggle with complex billing, long waits, or hurried, overbooked, stressed doctors running late or unavailable after hours.

Concierge practices can be set up as franchises, affiliations, or independent ownerships. Practices can be opened as concierge practices or they can transition to this service model from a more typical practice. There are many decisions to be considered prior to transitioning a practice into concierge service. Many who have made the transition find this new experience extremely rewarding, enabling them to be doctors who care for patients with focused, unhurried time and attention to quality personal care.

## Hospitalists

*Hospitalists*, sometimes called intensivists, are physicians whose primary focus is the care of hospitalized patients. Hospitalists' activities include patient care, research, teaching, and leadership related to hospital care. Recent research studies indicate that hospitalists decrease patient lengths of stay, hospital costs, and patient mortality rates while increasing patient satisfaction. This has galvanized the hospital medicine profession and spurred demand for hospitalists. Currently, there are approximately 15,000 hospitalists nationwide. This number is expected to grow to 30,000 by the end of the decade. The Society of Hospital Medicine was established in 1997 to support and enhance the practice of hospital medicine.

## *Other Options*

Other physicians find that a full-time or part-time focus on academic medicine, teaching, or research is more suited to their personality and interests. Some doctors are able to develop a practice working as consultants to corporations, structuring health care programs that will ultimately reduce a company's insurance costs. Whatever your interests or specialty as a physician, there are more options available to you than ever. Before you open an office, it may be worthwhile to explore some of them.

# STRUCTURING YOUR PRACTICE

There are two primary means of opening a new medical practice. The first is as a solo practitioner; the other is as a two-doctor or multiple-doctor practice. After you make that decision, you should determine the structure of your business. Depending on your needs and circumstances, your practice could be set up as a *sole proprietorship, partnership, corporation,* or one of the other limited liability forms of business now allowed in most states.

As you are deciding on the structure of your practice, it is helpful to reflect on your work habits both within and outside the practice of medicine. For example, have you been able to work alone on projects, get them organized, and take responsibility for their completion without involving the assistance of others? If so, then a solo practice might be easier for you than for others who work better as part of a team. If you examine your past activities and find that you work well with others and perhaps take leadership roles, then a multiple-physician practice may be the place for you.

When developing the focus of a new practice and its specialty, an overall philosophy is a necessary ingredient in your planning. For example, consider whether or not the practice is going to include a certain portion of its work to be pro bono. Will the practice have a policy of seeking out disabled employees? Will your practice be more than just a profit-making organization? All of these issues should be discussed among the beginning members of a practice, or considered in detail by the sole practitioner before the office opens its doors.

The practice's short-, medium-, and long-term goals are also an important part of initial planning. For example, a beginning doctor might plan to increase the number of physicians in the practice on an annual basis, or develop a certain level of patient activity per year. These goals form the basis for the compensation allocation provisions of the practice's governing documents. Since each of these goals has associated costs, they also require that you plan for the growth of your income. It must be remembered that professional liability remains regardless of the structure of the practice.

## SOLE PRACTITIONERS

Doctors who work well alone often find that a sole practice is best for them. However, practitioners have to be self-starters and self-organizers.

For doctors who are personally fulfilled by practicing alone, the advantages include freedom of decision making, freedom from wrangling over fees and distributions, and the personal satisfaction of achieving success by the use of their own wits. That sense of accomplishment is very important and a powerful motivator.

Sole practitioners have the disadvantage of not having partners or associates available to discuss medical or professional issues and get other opinions, which can be valuable in analyzing a medical problem. This is a good reason for sole practitioners to join a suite of doctors or rent space from other doctors, where they can easily exchange information.

Naturally, if you are a sole practitioner, all of the management functions fall upon your shoulders. Depending on your managerial and multitasking skills, you may see this as an advantage or a disadvantage.

A solo doctor who has an outside source of income—such as military retirement, early retirement, disability payments, or extra income from the family—may begin practice as a sole practitioner with the plan to expand the practice to include other doctors in the future.

# PARTNERSHIPS

You have to be brave to start a medical practice, and it makes sense to want others around you when you do. A partnership, which can have two or more doctor-partners, offers the advantage of having someone with whom to brainstorm, share the expenses, and expand your patient network. However, the main reason for entering a partnership is for financial benefit— to share the substantial costs of establishing and equipping a medical office.

When you start out with multiple doctors, the task of finding an office location can be complicated by multiple viewpoints on where the office should be located and what the costs should be. In some cases, a beginning doctor may contribute less in terms of cash or financial support than the others.

Another problem is dividing up the labor of managing the practice so that no one doctor is burdened with time spent on management. The allocation of administrative and management functions is crucial, because if any one of them breaks down, the whole organization suffers. When there are two or three physicians, the management of the practice can be shared or it can be done by one of the doctors with an adjustment of compensation for the time that is taken to handle such activities.

Management responsibilities are covered in more detail in Chapter 10, and include such tasks as supervising staff; hiring, training, and firing employees; dealing with the billing department and bookkeeper to make sure statements are sent, bills are paid on time, and the practice's financial affairs are managed properly; making sure that the accounts receivable are monitored; and, handling negotiations related to the office space, such as maintenance, parking, and improvement issues.

As the firm continues to grow, and most crucially if the practice has multiple partners, it will become necessary to have a partner devoted full-time to managing the practice. Your management plan should include the requirement that when the practice reaches its optimum size, one of the doctors will have to become the managing partner. Alternatively, doctors may be appointed to fill this position on a rotation basis, possibly for a year at a time.

Friendship and camaraderie are not sufficient bases for choosing the people who will help you begin your medical practice. The ability for partners to get along with each other is critical. Their work habits, personal integrity, and ability to attract clients are crucial considerations. You must examine, among other things, their technical skills, people skills, integrity, and track record.

You may want to look for a partner who is very different from you. Many duo practitioners are successful when one of them is more outgoing, gregarious, and comfortable with people, while the other is quiet, shy, and happy to work alone. This can be a very effective working team.

## Partnership Agreements

Before a partnership is formed, the partners must discuss the plans for developing the practice, operating the office, and deciding who is responsible for the management functions. Partnerships can be formed orally or in writing, though an oral agreement may lead to problems down the road. In today's climate, a well-drafted partnership agreement is essential. The partners should engage the services of a lawyer who specializes in such agreements, and pay the fee to get the expert advice and drafted documents.

The agreement covers essential areas, such as capital contributions, profit-sharing, and dissolution decisions regarding buy and sell agreements if one of the partners leaves. The partners must also establish standards for fee distributions within the practice, including the means of rewarding doctors for administrative and management responsibilities.

One of the most important parts of a partnership agreement is the area devoted to the expansion of the partnership and how new physicians will be brought into the practice.

# LIMITED LIABILITY PARTNERSHIPS

With multiple doctor practices, the standard partnership has been the most common form of medical practice until recently. In such partnerships, the doctors are entitled to an equal share of the income. They also jointly share the liabilities of the partnership, putting their personal assets on the line. A *limited liability partnership* (LLP) is a way of protecting partners. A partner in an LLP has limited liability for the obligations of the partnership or its liabilities to the partners or third parties.

In addition to uniform requirements, LLP determinations are established by statutory or regulatory law. Each jurisdiction may have special requirements for insurance protection for professional liability and other protections for patients' interests. A doctor may not avoid personal liability for the consequences of his or her professional errors and omissions, and jurisdictions may also require malpractice insurance or the execution of a personal guarantee.

The downside to organizing and qualifying as an LLP becomes more apparent when it is time for the partnership to terminate or dissolve. There may be both state and federal tax problems. All of these considerations must be understood before the LLP is formed.

# CORPORATIONS

The *professional corporation* is another form that the practice may take to protect the partners from liability. However, the primary advantage of the professional corporation is the establishment of pension plans and retirement plans.

Incorporating allows you to set aside pretax money for retirement funds. The monies contributed to retirement plans are deducted when determining the corporation's taxable income. The tax on those funds upon the worker's retirement is probably going to be lower than the tax at the time the money is earned. Tax benefits also include the option of retaining earnings for a lower corporate income tax rate. The corporation's ownership of automobiles and other large dollar items can also be a tax advantage for an individual.

*Does this apply to LLP or LLC also?*

The advantages of incorporating are primarily financial and tax-related, and may not be practical for a medical practice that is just getting started. A tax advisor—either a tax lawyer or a CPA—should be consulted before making the decision to incorporate, because the financial implications are substantial.

There are differences of opinion as to the threshold for incorporation, but there are two benchmarks to keep in mind.
1. If the individual doctor's income is below $500,000, incorporation is impractical.
2. If the medical practice has fewer than four principals, then incorporation is impractical.

## *Benefit Plans*

Corporations have the option of establishing pension plans as well as profit-sharing plans, which allow contributions from profits if the board of directors so desires. You can maximize the options and flexibility of the corporation by adopting both plans. The secret to success of such plans is the prudent adjustment of the monies involved and the added advantage that no income taxes are paid on those funds or their investment yields until the benefits are paid upon retirement or death.

The plans must be qualified under applicable requirements of the Internal Revenue Service and the Department of Labor. While partnerships and sole practitioners can also receive similar tax deductions for retirement plans, the important difference is the maximum limits on such deductions.

One characteristic of these plans is that a corporation must not discriminate in favor of the shareholders and must treat everyone equally. All employees must be covered under the corporate and Keogh retirement plans, although the benefits and the coverage are variable based upon the annual compensation and length of service of each employee.

Other advantages of incorporation are the options of establishing medical and dental plans, which pay up to 100% of all employee and dependent care, either through insurance premiums or fees for services. The corporation has the option of obtaining group term life insurance for each employee, currently up to about $50,000, and the premiums are deductible without causing taxable income to the employee or beneficiary of the policy. There are other options, such as sick pay and death and disability benefit plans, that the corporation may also obtain.

## *Transferring Ownership*

One of the important advantages of incorporating that has very little to do with tax issues is the management of the transfer of shares when expanding the corporation. The shares can be issued by the corporation and bought and sold under limited circumstances by members of the corporation. The relative monetary interest in the practice can be more easily identified and controlled. For example, the corporation may have a provision that the shares of the corporation can be sold only to those individuals who are invited or nominated to become shareholders in the practice by the practice's board of directors. This gives the practice the ability to determine with whom they are going to work and share their income.

This function is similar to that of a partnership, whereby one becomes a partner only when the other partners extend the invitation. That same personalized treatment is available even though the practice is incorporated. As the practice grows, this makes it a lot easier to bring in individual doctors or groups of doctors who are going to be added to a practice as a department.

Regardless of the mode or structure of the practice at the beginning, it is wise to prepare for the future and to know what options you have as you progress. If your plan is to remain a sole practitioner or a dual or very small practice, you still need to have some long-range view for the future. If your plan is to grow, then the tax and nontax advantages of incorporating become more important as the practice enlarges.

## Formalities of the Corporation

The formalities are the same for all corporations. Corporate minutes and records of board meetings must be kept, and the separation of corporation issues and personal issues must be meticulously recorded. The corporation is the party to all the practice's contracts, such as retainer agreements and contingency fee agreements.

The corporation is the provider of the services, not the individual doctor (although individual liability still applies). Doctors may not evade their professional and personal liability just because they are incorporated.

There are other financial obligations of the corporation, such as annual fees and the added expense for administration of the pension plans and the necessary tax deductions peculiar to the corporate mode. The Internal Revenue Service must recognize the corporation in order to allow all of the deductions to be taken, and that is why meticulous adherence to the rules is necessary.

The doctors employed by the corporation should have written employment agreements, with the salaries and employment benefits specifically spelled out. The compensation for the principals must have some rational relationship to the services they render.

## *Professional Liability*

As in a partnership, the principals in a professional corporation can be held to guarantee the liabilities of the others, within certain limits. A loan made to a corporation will almost always require the guarantee of one or more of the doctors, and the same is true for leases entered into by the corporation.

In a partnership, the partners may bear personal liability for such things as personal injury or property damage caused by an employee who is negligent or a defective condition of the premises. In a corporation, the comprehensive general liability policy issued to the corporation should cover such liability without the maximum exposure of the individual doctors' personal assets.

As with general partnerships, a professional corporation should have appropriate life insurance protection for the principals if one of them dies or becomes totally disabled. With the remaining principals as beneficiaries, the interest and the management of an enterprise is maintained within the confines of the practice.

Without such buy and sell agreements to protect the principals, intolerable problems could arise. When a principal dies or divorces without a provision protecting the remaining principals, the assets then go to a nonphysician beneficiary and the situation can become unduly complicated. These situations can be handled easily with a properly drafted set of incorporating documents and appropriate insurance policies.

# LLC OR SUBCHAPTER S CORPORATION

A limited liability company (LLC) is permitted in many states and in a corporate structure approved by the IRS. It has the advantage that corporate income may be *passed through* to the individual and not be taxed twice. The shareholder may not be liable for

*Does this apply to LLP also?*

the debts of the LLC. The LLC have many of the advantages of a partnership and a corporation.

A Subchapter S corporation is a corporate election that may be made for tax purposes with certain requirements. It may have no more than seventy-five shareholders, one class of stock held by individuals who are U.S. residents, and a calendar-year fiscal basis. Similar to the LLC, the income tax liability in an S corporation is *passed through* to the individual shareholders.

You should consult your tax advisor or attorney for advice as to the best legal structure of your business and the advantages and disadvantages of each.

## FIRM AGREEMENTS

You or your partners may be opening your own office after leaving another medical practice. If so, you must examine the employment contracts from the former practices, which may inhibit the establishment of a competing practice. In most jurisdictions, covenants not to compete are disfavored, but it does not mean they are absolutely unenforceable. It just means that they are enforceable under certain circumstances.

For example, partnership agreements for medical practices may have provisions that govern the ability of practice partners or shareholders to compete with the practice itself. This does not apply to employed doctors. This supports the strong public policy in favor of allowing patients to have the right to choose their doctor without being frustrated by restrictive agreements.

The different treatment of shareholders and partners is brought about because they have financial interests in the practice that they want to leave. The corporation or partnership has a right to determine who will receive the departing member's financial interest and to make financial restrictions apply to its members.

These arrangements are generally negotiable. Mediation is one of the best ways to resolve any disputes of corporate members and partners leaving their practices to practice elsewhere.

# chapter three:
# Business Formation Fundamentals

There are certain fundamental actions that must be taken in order for you to open your doors as a business, and particularly as a professional medical practice. This chapter provides a checklist that covers the start-up items that are easy to overlook. Some of the items on the checklist can be done simultaneously, and the order of importance can be changed somewhat to accommodate your circumstances.

## IMPORTANT PRELIMINARIES

- ❏ Write your business plan. (see Chapter 2.)
- ❏ Obtain your business license. This will introduce you to the tax authorities for your locality, whether it be a city, a county, or both. You can expect them to come around within the first year or two of your operation to examine your premises to see if what you are reporting as income is probably true. You will need a license to start any business, and you must have an address. If you have not obtained premises yet, you can use your home address, although for privacy purposes, this is a less desirable choice. A post office box is not usually an acceptable

address. The business address can be changed as many times as you like.

❏ Register a fictitious business name, or *doing business as* (DBA), if you are using a fictitious name (a clinic name, for example) and your jurisdiction requires it.

❏ Establish your office so that you have an address and a place for your telephone. This is the time when you should decide whether you want to share clinic space in a suite with others, obligate yourself to a long-term lease, or rent space on a month-to-month basis. Look for a space that will be suitable for at least two years.

❏ Negotiate lease or rental terms, including parking for doctors, staff, and patients.

❏ Interview and select a consultant who can help you make decisions about your computer system and decide whether you will use *Electronic Health Records* (EHR). (see Chapter 5.) Your decisions about computer hardware and software can affect your office layout as well as your selection of office furniture, telephone systems, and paper file storage requirements.

❏ Set up your telephone system. Make sure that the system has all the features that you and your staff will need, including local and long distance service, mute, conferencing, multiple lines (including a dedicated fax line), intercom (including phone sets in examination rooms), hands-free options, and do-not-disturb controls. You may want to purchase an earloop (such as Office Rover) that allows you to move around while you are talking on the phone.

❏ Decide how you will handle after-hours calls. There are many options for tracking and paging on-call doctors. Ask your telephone consultant for information and talk to established medical professionals in your area for recommendations on reliable medical answering services.

❑ Record a personal and office voice mail message. Even if you have office staff and an answering service, there may be times when all lines are busy and a patient has to hear a recorded message. Your office message should clearly state the doctor's name and instruct callers what to do in case of a medical emergency, who to call if you are on vacation, and what information to provide when the caller leaves a message. Listen to the message and re-record it until it is clear and professional, without hesitations, "ums," or other confusing sounds. Have a friend or family member call and listen to the recording to make sure both the sound and the content of the message are clear. Once your practice gets going, check the message regularly to make sure that it is accurate.

❑ Establish your email address, and if appropriate, your Web address. You can arrange for these addresses before your computer is installed. You will need them for your business cards.

❑ Set up bank accounts, including office, personal, and safe-deposit boxes. If your practice is set up as a corporation, you will need a resolution from the board of directors to do all of these things. If you are a partnership, you will need a signed order from the managing partner or one of the general partners. If you are operating with a fictitious business name, you will need accounts in that name.

❑ Obtain credit card capability as a courtesy to patients who prefer that method of payment.

❑ Order business cards, stationery, prescription pads, and announcements. You may be used to doing most of your communication by email, and that will probably continue. However, you will also find it necessary to correspond with other physicians, professional associations, publications, and patients. Your stationery should be appropriately professional.

❑ Obtain the services of a reliable and qualified accountant or CPA who will set up your accounting and bookkeeping systems.

❑ Obtain a federal tax identification number, an employer identification number (EIN), and any other tax-related identification that your state may require. Your accountant may be able to assist with this process.

❑ Obtain the services of a knowledgeable insurance broker who specializes in medical practices and who can advise you regarding personal and professional insurance policies. In addition to various forms of practice insurance, you may also need special coverage for your office facility.

❑ Apply to state and local medical associations that may be necessary or beneficial to your practice.

❑ Decide if you want the expense of medical newspapers, magazines, or specialty publications. If you are sharing an office, you may be able to circulate copies of these publications and share their subscription costs. You may also wish to subscribe to online news and research services.

# chapter four:
# Office Design, Layout, and Furnishings

Once your location is selected, you want to look at the office with an eye toward utility and aesthetics. Furnishing your office with antiques, plush rugs, and expensive oil paintings may be your goal, but such capital outlay can be substantial and far more than is necessary for your purposes. Simple furniture and carpeting is quite acceptable for most practices. Whatever your style choices, furniture should be well cared for, comfortable, and practical for long hours of sitting.

Your choices can range from simple to extravagant. The furniture for the reception area, doctors' offices, and staff spaces can be purchased, leased, or rented. In general, companies lease furniture for a year or longer, while rentals are usually for less than a year. Your decision will depend on the finances of the practice and your short-term plans. If you are opening a temporary office while you complete work on a permanent location, leasing or renting furniture may be ideal. Talk with your CPA or tax advisor as you consider your furniture expenses. You would not want your leather sofa to affect your cash flow or your ability to borrow working capital.

New office furniture is always an option. Furniture stores often give favorable credit terms. As your practice expands, the furniture dealer is useful in obtaining additional pieces consistent with the price range and style you have already established.

Be aware that all new furniture is designed to look its best in the showroom. The real test of quality is how a piece of furniture stands up to daily wear and tear. If you are working with a decorator, ask about fabrics and fill for upholstered furniture. Will you be able to spot clean the sofa if someone spills coffee or bleeds on it? Will the cushions start sagging after a year in the waiting room? Even with constant use, well-constructed, high-quality furniture, which of course costs more up front, will far outlast the less expensive models—even if they look nearly identical in the showroom.

Office furniture can also be purchased through used furniture dealers, auction houses, and the Internet. Auctions may provide opportunities for obtaining fine furniture—even antiques—at very reasonable prices. The entire office need not be furnished all at once, but important pieces can be added over a period of time.

One of the most important pieces—and something that should not be skimped on—is the office chair. Chairs for doctors and staff may be your single most important acquisition as you furnish your office. Seating should provide excellent support and ergonomic positioning suitable for the work being done over the course of many hours each day. The chair's size, structure, firmness, upholstery, arm height and width, and adjustability should all be taken into consideration. Never purchase a chair until you have sat in it, preferably at a desk setup similar to the one where it will be used. Also, do not assume that the same chair will work for every desk in the office. In some places, such as computer stations or examination rooms, you may want rolling chairs without arms; in other places, such as doctors' offices and reception stations, chairs with arms will provide greater comfort.

Newspaper classified ads can also be a good source of information regarding furniture—not just for the furniture itself, but for dealers who may have a wide selection of office furniture, new or used, that will save you time as you shop.

## WORK SPACE PLANNING

Depending on the nature of your practice, you will have specific work space requirements. In addition to the doctor's office, waiting room, and staff space, you may need examination rooms (with plumbing, in some cases) and space for specialized equipment. Privacy and confidentiality are critical in your practice, and the doctor's office and examination rooms should provide sound barriers so that other patients and staff cannot overhear conversations.

Having the right kind of furniture—comfortable, practical, and ergonomically correct—and placing it efficiently is essential in running a smooth office. Built-in furniture typically makes more efficient use of space, while freestanding furniture allows flexibility and more creative design choices.

Even if you are on a tight budget, a designer can help you establish effective work flow and traffic patterns for your office. Such planning assures that doors and hallways are wide enough to accommodate wheelchairs, that staff members can move around the office without disrupting one another, that cabinets and drawers can be opened without blocking passageways, and that frequently used supplies and equipment are readily at hand. By determining your traffic pattern early, you can continue to add furniture as your budget allows.

Items that you use daily should be within arm's reach and everything else should be put away. A simple exercise can help: sit in your chair, stretch out your arms, and rotate slowly around in the swivel chair. You should be able to put your hands on frequently used items, such as telephone, stapler, tape dispenser, calendar, computer keyboard, and other necessary supplies, without reaching or bending.

The doctor's office should be a pleasant place to work, suitable for long hours. In many medical offices in large buildings, the need to economize space has mandated that doctors have very small offices, furnished with little more than a desk, a chair, and two patients' chairs. A small table holding flowers and pictures can make even a very small office more attractive.

---

### Doctor's Office Checklist

❑ Desk approximately six feet wide with non-scratch and spill-proof surface
❑ High-backed chair with wheels or rollers
❑ Suitable task lighting for desk
❑ At least two comfortable chairs for patients or other visitors
❑ Large, clear floor pad for chair in carpeted office
❑ Small conference table, if space allows
❑ Floor lamp
❑ Live plants
❑ Wastebasket
❑ Table or special desk for computer
❑ Bookshelves
❑ Framed diplomas and awards
❑ Personal photos

---

# THE WAITING ROOM

The waiting room is the first thing that people see and a place where patients and their family members will have to spend periods of time. The statement made by the décor and furniture of the waiting room is very important, and should not look cheap or skimpy. While you do not want your patients to think that they are paying for opulent offices, you want to convey a subtle message of solid success, and provide a waiting area that is homey and comfortable enough to allay anxiety.

The reception area should have comfortable seating. Individual chairs are more expensive than a couch or two, but people in the waiting room will be more comfortable in chairs. A coffee table or side tables, with adequate lighting, can offer magazines and other reading materials so that people have something to focus on while they are waiting for their appointment. If space is limited, a wall-mounted magazine or brochure rack is useful. A painting or two, and perhaps some decorative fabric or small sculptures, will set a tone of tasteful professionalism that will help your patients feel at ease. Live plants or a fish tank are also attractive additions to the waiting room, but require regular maintenance. Some doctors offer coffee or tea in their waiting rooms.

---

## Basic Waiting Area Checklist

- ❏ Comfortable chairs
- ❏ Hat and coat rack
- ❏ Umbrella stand
- ❏ Coffee table
- ❏ Reading lights
- ❏ Side table
- ❏ Live plants
- ❏ Fish tank
- ❏ Magazine rack
- ❏ Brochure rack
- ❏ Coffee service

---

# SUPPORT STAFF AREA

The area for the office manager, nurses, doctor's assistants, and other staff should be separate from the public areas and utility rooms to promote efficient work, preserve confidentiality, and minimize overheard conversations. Office furniture stores or your decorator will help you determine what furniture you should use in the staff area, but you should have a basic desk with a computer, telephone, chair, file drawers, and shelves.

# COMMON SPACES

Lighting throughout the office should be both general and task-specific. Arrange lighting to minimize glare and reflections on computer monitors. To reduce electricity costs, you may want to install motion detector on/off switches in rooms that are not occupied full-time, such as storage areas and restrooms.

Noise control is critical in medical offices. Conversations and equipment sounds can travel throughout the office and disturb everyone within earshot. Carpeting, upholstery, and fabric-covered walls or partitions help to muffle sound and reduce noise, but you may need to get more efficient soundproofing. You should also establish an office policy about the use of hands-free and all phones, radios, and other personal electronic sound equipment, as well as sound levels on office computers.

Somewhere in the office there should be storage facilities for client files as well as office and sanitation supplies.

An employee lounge—even a very small space—gives those who share the office a place to socialize and communicate within the workplace without disturbing coworkers. This can be extremely valuable in maintaining high morale. Coffee equipment, a soft drink dispenser, and a refrigerator should be adequate to support staff needs as well as to provide for the occasional office guest.

---

## Employee Lounge Checklist

- ❑ Coffee maker and hot water dispenser with coffee and tea supplies
- ❑ Microwave
- ❑ Refrigerator
- ❑ Table and four to six utility chairs
- ❑ Cups, plates, and bowls
- ❑ Paper towels and dispenser
- ❑ Knives, forks, spoons, and carving knife
- ❑ Dish washing supplies
- ❑ Hand soap and dispenser
- ❑ Water dispenser—hot and cold
- ❑ Cabinets to lock valuables
- ❑ Basic tool box, pliers, screwdriver, hammer
- ❑ Live plants

# FILING SYSTEMS

One of the areas that should not be neglected in setting up an office is a filing system. If you are using a space planner, he or she can help you devise a system that works in your space, and office supply companies will be able to help you find the necessary components. The medical practice management section of the American Medical Association also provides help in determining what kind of filing system you should have and the relative costs of each one. Even if you decide to initiate an Electronic Health Record system from the outset of your practice, you will still need space to file paper, and in some cases, film records.

The filing system that you choose at the outset can follow you throughout your practice, so you should start with a system that can be expanded in the future in almost an unlimited fashion. The purging of files is something that you should provide for in your office procedures.

# DÉCOR

You may wish to get expert advice from an interior decorator. A well thought-out color scheme and the attractive placement of furniture can make a relatively plain medical practice into a pleasant, charming, and relaxing place for you, your staff, and your patients. If you cannot afford a decorator, there are other ways of getting such help. For example, if you buy furniture or accessories from department stores, you can take advantage of their free decorator services.

If you are going to be setting up your office in a shared office suite, the furniture will be provided and charges included in the monthly rent. Décor is usually handled by professional decorators and is generally attractive and neutral enough to appeal to a variety of tastes.

Your overall décor may also be affected by the type of practice you have. For example, a pediatrician's office might use a vibrant color scheme and add some small-scale furniture and a play area, while a sports medicine practice might want to invest in a waiting room television to broadcast sports news.

The overall attitude of people who work in the office will be affected by the color scheme, the quality of the furniture, the decorations, and other aspects of the office. Sculptures and paintings that are done by someone connected with the practice can be excellent conversation pieces. However, keep in mind that if you put one relative's artwork in your office and not that of another, you may create a family problem. You may be able to begin your personal art collection and obtain pieces of art at relatively low prices from an artist who is also beginning a professional life.

Doctors and staff should be given the opportunity to display some items that are unique to them as a part of their office décor. This should be done with reasonable limitations. For example, overgrown plants that are intruding on adjacent spaces should be trimmed, and areas that are visible to patients should be kept uncluttered and consistent with the office design scheme. (Once your practice is established, you may want to hire a plant maintenance service to assure that all office flora stays healthy and attractive.)

The limitation on personal decorations should be explained in the staff manual, so that staff are not embarrassed to discover that their décor has caused a problem. Such personal issues can demand unusual tact and diplomacy.

## MAINTAINING THE OFFICE

Once you have set up your office, you need to make sure that it is maintained consistently. A regular cleaning service should be supplemented with additional care, such as carpet cleaning. Someone on your staff should watch for worn or stained carpet, upholstery, and wall coverings, which can communicate the wrong message in even the most successful medical practice. Parts of the office that are accessible to patients, including the waiting room, restrooms, and examination rooms, must be checked throughout the day for cleanliness and to assure that patients have not left behind any personal belongings.

In addition, you will need to establish a contract with a hazardous material disposal service for medical waste disposal. Your landlord or local medical association may be able to provide information about available services.

# chapter five:
# Equipment

Any business needs basic equipment to be able to operate. The initial expenses for such things can be substantial. Your medical practice will require both general office equipment and medical equipment. For the new office, it makes sense to explore your options before making any selections. A list of the basic components needed as you set up your office is on page 43. An office supplies list is on page 45.

## TO BUY, LEASE, OR RENT

As with furniture, equipment can be purchased, leased, or rented. That decision will depend upon the finances of the practice and the availability of discounts from vendors. Equipment costs can affect your balance sheet and should be discussed with your tax advisor as you determine the capital outlay that you will be required to make in beginning your medical practice.

Leasing may be a good way of obtaining the latest, state-of-the-art equipment. When improved equipment becomes available, the lease can be renegotiated and the equipment can be upgraded. If the equipment is purchased, your only option is to sell it or trade it in for new equipment. Purchasing equipment requires capital, whereas leasing may only depend upon your credit rating.

Depending upon the nature of your practice, you may require certain pieces of large equipment in order to open your office. Consultants in health care obtained through specialty colleges, academies, associations, and local hospitals can usually help you get the necessary information you need. A leasing broker may also be helpful as many vendors offer leasing options attractive to physicians with less capital. Also seek advice on equipment from your seasoned colleagues.

Large office equipment, such as photocopiers, can be obtained from used-equipment dealers. This is an area where a consultant can be extremely valuable. When a practice closes down or upgrades its equipment, used items may be made available. Sometimes, all you have to do is to take over the payments on a leased piece of equipment.

An extensive market in reconditioned copiers provides a large cost-savings opportunity for doctors. A new copy machine, which may obligate the doctor or practice to a $30,000 lease, may be obtained second-hand with warranty for as little as $7,000 to $10,000, or leased at a comparable monthly expense. As medical offices rely increasingly upon electronic files, the need for a large, high-demand copier is likely to diminish, even as your practice grows. A small model, even a desktop copier, available for hundreds instead of thousands of dollars, may be adequate for your needs. Like computer printers, copiers are rated by the number of copies they are designed to make for optimum use. Your office manager should be able to help you determine this number so you can purchase or lease the equipment that is right for your office.

If you assume the lease of a medical office that has closed down or is moving, you can gain valuable access to resources for your medical practice. The medical office management section of your local medical association can help you make contact with practices that are closing. Medical book salespeople, drug company sales representatives, or office materials sales representatives can also be helpful, because they have access to many medical practices and can tell you which ones are downsizing, expanding, or shutting down, and where furniture and collections of books are for sale.

With each significant acquisition, either personal or for the practice, you should carefully compare the cost of purchasing with the cost of leasing. The lease is likely to be higher in total payout, because it will include interest, taxes, and other charges that the leasing company has to pay. Purchased equipment may seem less expensive, but the cost of interest on borrowed money should be factored into your calculations.

## Basic Office Equipment Checklist

- ❏ Telephone system
- ❏ Fax machine
- ❏ Copy machine
- ❏ Computers
- ❏ Scanner
- ❏ Fast black and white laser printer
- ❏ Portable tape recorders
- ❏ Dictating unit
- ❏ Transcription unit
- ❏ Fireproof safe for important documents
- ❏ Postage meter
- ❏ Paper cutter
- ❏ Staplers and staple removers
- ❏ Filing cabinets
- ❏ Check protector

## Examination Room and Lab Supplies Checklist

**NOTE:** *Supplies for these areas will depend largely upon the nature of your practice. This is a very general list of some of the most basic supplies.*

❑ Examination table
❑ Examination table covers
❑ Examination lights
❑ Patient gowns
❑ Pillows and cases
❑ Doctor's chair or stool
❑ Patient chair or two
❑ Step stool
❑ Scale
❑ Height measuring rod
❑ Mayo instrument stand
❑ Gloves
❑ Sphygmomanometer
❑ Thermometers
❑ Syringes
❑ Refrigerator
❑ Autoclave
❑ Ultrasonic cleaner
❑ Bandage materials
❑ Diagnostic tests as appropriate
❑ Practice-specific medical supplies, tools, and equipment
❑ Lab coats and doctor's coat
❑ Wastebaskets and hazardous material disposal
❑ Emergency cleaning supplies
❑ First aid supplies
❑ Automated External Defibrillator (AED)
❑ Emergency cart as needed for your practice
❑ Wheelchair and crutches

# Office Supplies Checklist

**NOTE:** *Discuss office needs with an experienced medical office manager.*

❑ Stationery
❑ Envelopes, including manila
❑ Business cards
❑ Appointment cards
❑ Prescription pads
❑ Pens and pencils
❑ Felt-tipped markers
❑ Two-hole and three-hole punches
❑ Telephone message books
❑ Rubber stamps and ink pads
❑ Paper clips, stapler, and staples
❑ Scissors
❑ Files
❑ Check books
❑ Address labels
❑ Postage stamps
❑ Copier paper and lined note pads
❑ Toner for printers and copiers
❑ Other

## SUPPLY INVENTORY

| Reorder | Item | Total # | Date Ordered Source/Initials | Date Received | Check by (Initials) | Usage Tracking | Misc/Notes |
|---------|------|---------|------------------------------|---------------|---------------------|----------------|------------|
|         |      |         |                              |               |                     |                |            |
|         |      |         |                              |               |                     |                |            |
|         |      |         |                              |               |                     |                |            |
|         |      |         |                              |               |                     |                |            |
|         |      |         |                              |               |                     |                |            |
|         |      |         |                              |               |                     |                |            |
|         |      |         |                              |               |                     |                |            |
|         |      |         |                              |               |                     |                |            |

# TELEPHONES

Beyond the furnishings, one of your most important office tools is the telephone system. To provide essential communication with patients, other doctors, hospitals, pharmacies, answering services, cell phones, and your on-call procedure, your telephone system must be compatible with your computer. Before you install a major phone system in your new office, talk with a knowledgeable technology consultant.

If you will be installing a multiple-line, multiple-instrument system in your office, discuss with the consultant your options for leasing the equipment. Leasing may give you a better opportunity to expand and upgrade as new features become available or as your practice grows and new equipment becomes necessary.

Your office should have a minimum of three telephone lines and two telephone numbers. One of the lines and one of the numbers should be dedicated for your fax. All of your office work stations should also be equipped to handle high-speed data transfer, including wireless. Telephone features should include intercom, speaker phone, mute, hands-free, hold, do not disturb, and conferencing.

To help you make your phone system a useful tool, develop a *Telephone Intake Form* like the one on page 48. This will ensure that vital, but easily overlooked, information is obtained.

## Communications Checklist

❑ Obtain telephone and fax numbers, as well as email addresses

❑ Obtain dedicated lines for these numbers and reserve a domain name for a website

❑ Obtain a dedicated line for your computer

❑ Obtain cell phones and make certain that the numbers are portable from vendor to vendor

❑ Obtain the highest speed Internet service available within your budget

❑ Engage a printer for stationery, business cards, announcements, prescription pads, invoices, and other printed material

❑ Make certain that you utilize phone company services as much as your budget allows, including call forwarding, call waiting, speakerphone, remote access to call forwarding, teleconferencing, and caller ID

## Telephone Intake Form

Date and time of call: _____

Caller's full name: _____

Telephone numbers, including fax and cell: _____

_____

Brief description of the problem: _____

_____

Caller's home address: _____

_____

_____

Appointment date and time: _____

# Telephone Log Sheet

Triage Nurse _____

Date _____

| Name | Phone # | Time | Problem | Recommend |
|------|---------|------|---------|-----------|
|      |         |      |         |           |
|      |         |      |         |           |
|      |         |      |         |           |
|      |         |      |         |           |
|      |         |      |         |           |
|      |         |      |         |           |
|      |         |      |         |           |
|      |         |      |         |           |
|      |         |      |         |           |

# GEARING UP: COMPUTER HARDWARE AND SOFTWARE

Whether you are a tech-savvy physician or one who will forever prefer your unreadable prescription scrawl, your new medical practice will require a diverse array of hardware and software. The computers that you choose for yourself and your staff may be the single most important technical decision that you are going to have to make. Do not attempt it alone, and do not rely on the salesperson in your local computer store to advise you. Seek the expertise of a computer consultant who has both deep technical knowledge and particular experience in the needs of medical offices. Ask your professional colleagues or your local medical association for recommendations and interview the consultant before commencing, just as you would any potential employee. Be cautious of consultants whose solutions are based on equipment that you must purchase from them.

This book cannot offer exhaustive details on computer systems, but this chapter provides some guidelines that will assist you as you make your decisions. In general, you should look for a number of qualities in your computer system: speed, memory, expandability, flexibility, compatibility, networking, security, and backup. You want to build a system that reflects the way you actually work and is easily adaptable as your practice grows. While hardware and software are quickly obsolete, look for solid, proven systems that can be upgraded as necessary.

You may have a computer that you used throughout college and medical school, and you may feel comfortable with that system. Ask your consultant whether it is practical to open up your medical office with that equipment. Discuss your preferences, the relative merits and compatibility of PCs and Macs for physicians, and the essential hardware and software for your business. (Be sure to read the section on Electronic Health Records on page 58 before you start shopping.)

Computer choices are personal, but they are also driven by the nature of your practice. Keep in mind that the doctors and staff who will be using the equipment may have a wide range of technical expertise. The system should accommodate everyone comfortably—it should allow your computer-savvy clerks and secretaries to speed through documents using all available short-cuts, and also be user-friendly for the doctor who types at home using the hunt-and-peck method.

While it may be tempting to equip your office for the staff you envision acquiring over the next five years, it makes more sense to start small and expand gradually—an idle work station can easily become obsolete before someone sits at it. Set up your office for the doctors and staff you have now and anticipate hiring in the next quarter. Test that equipment and make sure it meets your needs. Then, as you increase the size of your staff, add components, always providing the fastest new equipment to the most skilled users.

As you are planning your computer system, consider carefully the way you actually work. For example, do you do a lot of your work on a laptop? Do you send and receive email and keep important information in a handheld device, such as a Palm or BlackBerry? Do you prefer to dictate rather than type? Do you handwrite drafts on paper or on an electronic tablet? Do you use speech recognition software? Do you use videoconferencing? The computer world is full of dazzling gadgets; make sure the ones you purchase are practical and useful for your business.

## *Computer Hardware*

Depending upon the size of your practice, your system will include a number of servers, computers, monitors, printers, scanners, projectors, backup power supplies, and other external components, such as handheld devices, mice, backup drives, and so on. While your computer system will require a considerable outlay of cash, high performance systems are less and less expensive as newer models appear on the scene.

Long-term usefulness is critical. It is better to spend a little more on a solid, mainstream system than to look for the lowest-priced model and risk lost data or disrupted service when it crashes and you are forced to replace it. Though the prices may make it tempting, avoid used equipment, which is often underpowered and not easily upgraded. An efficient new system that has adequate capacity for your needs can be purchased for a reasonable cost, and it will be covered by warranty.

Your office system should accommodate both desktop and laptop computers. For you, a docking station with monitor and full-size keyboard may be more efficient than a desktop model; your office staff may find desktop systems more practical. However, if you will be implementing Electronic Health Records from the outset, doctors and staff may prefer a wireless system that allows laptop computers to be moved easily from desk to examination room and back.

Look for speed, power, and memory capacity as you are building your system. Get a computer with the fastest processor, clock rate (expressed in gigahertz, GHz), random-access memory (RAM) (expressed in megabytes, MB), and hard disk capacity (expressed in gigabytes, GB). Consider which elements will allow you the most power and flexibility as your practice grows—and resolve yourself to the knowledge that as soon as you have purchased your system, a faster one will come onto the market. Your consultant should be able to advise you on the best operating system (for example, Windows XP or MAC OS-X) for your needs.

Purchase the largest monitors you can afford—nothing smaller than 17-inch screens. While flat-screen monitors are still more expensive, they free up valuable desktop real estate and are both practical and handsome.

Your system should have broadband connectivity—Ethernet or wireless—to allow Internet access, email, and other forms of networking, and you may want a modem as backup. Even a small office must have a networked computer system that allows the physicians and staff to share files. This becomes more critical as you introduce Electronic Health Records (EHR) to your practice.

Your system should also come equipped with a powerful firewall for security, often part of the operating system (and be sure your office computer person regularly installs the necessary patches to keep the system current). CD/DVD burners are very practical, as are front-of-computer USB ports.

Document scanners enable paper documents (such as signed permission forms, advance directives, letters, etc.) to be scanned into the office network and added to a patient's file. *Optical character reading* (OCR) software associated with scanners translates scanned documents into text files. This will be especially valuable if you need to convert paper files to Electronic Health Records. Whether you store old files in electronic or paper form, an efficient and easily understood indexing system should be established to make sure that files can be retrieved if they are needed.

As your practice becomes increasingly dependent upon the computer system for everything from recording and retrieving prescription information to billing and carrying out medical research, a significant system failure can be very costly and disruptive. A backup power source, known as an *uninterrupted power supply* (UPS), is essential to protect the system from power failures.

A data backup system that automatically copies and stores files is also critical to the security of your practice. You should establish a backup protocol, including how frequently backups are made, where and how they are stored, and for how long they are kept before erasing and rerecording. Your backup system is only useful if it is consistently maintained and monitored.

If you do any teaching or anticipate making presentations, consider adding a digital projector to your system. Compact projectors can be connected to a laptop computer and used with PowerPoint to display documents and photographs to audiences. Video projectors permit documents to be displayed on a screen without having been scanned and stored into the computer. Be sure to stock spare bulbs and instruct projector users in proper system use and replacement of bulbs.

## Computer Software

Your computer's software allows you and your staff to carry out the scores of necessary tasks that comprise your business, such as scheduling appointments, recording patient data, accounting, billing, email, and many other tasks.

As with the purchase of hardware, it makes sense to acquire the latest software that your budget will allow. Stick with mainstream programs and update them regularly. Although you may eagerly await the newest software releases, it is not necessarily in your practice's best interest to be one of the first users of a new software program. You want to spend your time working efficiently rather than trying to solve the vendor's problems. Most critically, make sure that the programs you select are compatible with each other to streamline operations and eliminate the duplication of work.

Software programs constitute the heart of your medical recordkeeping, research, and communication, and there are certain ones that you should have when you start. Many of the vital and desirable programs for your practice are incorporated into EHR systems, so you should explore the EHR option before you start purchasing separate software packages. (see page 58.) In addition, *medical practice management* (MPM) software, which should be integrated with EHR, expands the capabilities of your office system. The five programs that you must have to begin your practice are the following.

1. Word processing software—which is used to prepare correspondence, reports, and other documents—is a useful place to begin. The standard cutting, pasting, copying, and other editing features of word processing programs are supplemented by the ability to number pages and paragraphs, and to prepare tables of contents. You can also combine graphics with text and create stationery and labels. Off-the-shelf computers may come with word processing software already installed. Make sure it is compatible with your other systems and works effectively for you before you start building new documents.

2. Billing software is essential and your system should have the capability of expanding and improving as your firm grows. It can produce invoices, statements, and other financial information, such as costs on a specific matter. Billing services are now available online, which allows you to bypass the software, and billing is an essential

component of EHR. Billing software should be integrated with *Current Procedural Terminology®* (CPT), as well as insurance codes, HMO/PPO fee schedules, billing cycle information, electronic remittance options, and electronic claims submissions. (See detailed billing information in Chapter 11.)

3. Accounting software ties in directly with your billing system, giving you access to the general ledger, accounts payable, cash balance, accounts receivable, and budgets. Your accountant can access your financial information easily so you do not have to provide this information at the last minute for the preparation of your tax returns.

4. Virus protection software is critical, and must be updated because new viruses constantly threaten the very heart of your office systems. The software finds and removes viruses that might get into your system and can be programmed to check each entry that you put into your computer, survey the hard drive of your computer, and monitor email messages to determine if they contain a virus. Newer antivirus software also contains anti-spam, anti-spyware, and anti-adware software programs, which are essential to your system's security.

5. While tape backup software has been the gold standard for data backup and storage, new disk- and virtual disk-based systems may offer a faster, more reliable backup. Whichever you choose, backup software is only as reliable as the staff responsible for its operation—it will not change tapes for you. The backup system must be monitored routinely, with someone on your staff having that responsibility as part of their job description. Make sure you understand how backed-up files are retrieved, how long they are maintained, and whether they are overwritten by new files or otherwise destroyed.

The software mentioned above supports many of the functions that you will find necessary in starting your practice. Some of them overlap and most will be integrated in your EHR system.

Your computer consultant or your technician should be able to advise you on the necessary hardware and software upgrades to keep your system current. It is his or her job to keep up with the marketplace, and you should take advantage of his or her expertise. Generally speaking, software products should be evaluated for upgrading approximately every two to three years. Exceptions to this are virus protection programs, which need to be monitored and upgraded frequently. Practice-specific programs should be upgraded semiannually.

## DAY-TO-DAY OPERATIONS

Your computer consultant will be able to advise you on the setup of your system, but you will also need day-to-day support for a variety of technical issues that arise. While a physician or staff person may be able to assist with minor computer-related problems, a computer technician who can respond on very short notice should also be available to resolve infrequent, but potentially vexing, computer failures that will arise. In smaller practices, a contract maintenance service should be engaged. As with any service business, obtain references before allowing a technician to repair or make significant alterations to your computer system.

Along with establishing other computer and office protocols, you will need to establish a training protocol for doctors and staff to assure that expensive hardware and software are used properly. A skilled staff person, an outside consultant, or a training school can handle this task.

The practice of medicine is not only labor intensive, but also equipment and paper intensive. You and your patients will benefit if you take the time to investigate, purchase, and install the best equipment that you can afford.

The establishment of your office computer system is one of the most important things you will do at the outset of your practice. If you find yourself dealing with a system that has become obsolete soon after you have installed it, you will find it extremely expensive and cumbersome to make a change. The time and money you spend up front will pay off in your long-term satisfaction with your system.

## ELECTRONIC HEALTH RECORDS

Just a generation ago, many physicians starting into private practice had to confront an unfamiliar piece of office equipment: a computer. Today it is almost unimaginable that a student could make it through high school and college, let alone medical school, without a computer. Still, that does not mean that a physician's electronic worries are over. These days, those worries take the shape of Electronic Health Records (EHR).

About 20% of physicians use EHR technology today—a growing number that probably reflects an increasing comfort with electronic media in general. With a price tag approaching $50,000, it is not surprising that hospitals and large group practices, with more available capital, are more likely to adopt the technology than small practices or sole practitioners.

As EHR is more widely adopted, package prices are dropping and software developers are coming up with new systems and lots of bells and whistles to make electronic recordkeeping easier and more attractive. Today, there are more than two hundred

EHR vendors in the marketplace, and that number could easily double. As options increase, it becomes more challenging to select a system that will be an investment as useful in five or ten years as it is today.

All EHR systems are not the same. In fact, even the terminology is somewhat confusing, with *electronic health record, electronic medical record, virtual health record, personal medical record,* and *electronic patient record* being used almost interchangeably. The *Institute of Medicine* (IOM) has considered the problem and defined criteria and uses of EHR. Very briefly, according to the IOM criteria, EHR must improve patient safety, support the delivery of effective patient care, facilitate management of chronic conditions, improve efficiency, and be feasible to implement. The IOM-defined uses of EHR systems are as follows.

Primary Uses:
- patient care delivery;
- patient care management;
- patient care support processes;
- financial and other administrative processes; and,
- patient self-management.

Secondary Uses:
- education;
- regulation;
- research;
- public health and homeland security; and,
- policy support.

In practical terms, the resources of an integrated EHR system are almost unlimited. From accessing patient records and test results to communicating with other providers and with patients themselves, EHR streamlines office procedures and can reduce the errors of manual recordkeeping. Even more promising is the ability of EHR systems to track treatments and show care management outcomes. Once it is installed, and once office personnel are trained, the system should easily fulfill the IOM criteria.

Selecting the right EHR system and features is far more demanding than choosing a one-size-fits-all personal computer. There are books on the subject as well as a number of online resources that may be able to help by making system recommendations to meet a physician's specific practice needs. It is not possible to cover the subject thoroughly in a few pages of this book, but the following provides some general guidelines to aid your selection process.

- Do not outsource your purchase decisions. While your trusted office manager may be extremely competent at selecting other office equipment, including computers, your EHR system will be something you use day in and day out. It needs to be comfortable for you and needs to meet your immediate and long-term goals.
- Do not assume that what works for a professional colleague will work for you. It is always helpful to get opinions and recommendations, but the system that works for someone else—even someone in the same specialty—will not necessarily be the best solution for you.
- Make sure that the system you select is fully functional (integrated) with any other programs you are currently using and that it interacts smoothly with the systems of the individuals and services you communicate with regularly (such as radiology, pharmacies, laboratories, consulting physicians, etc.). Individual components should be able to operate on their own and as part of an integrated system.
- Look ahead. You may be opening your office with one or two doctors, but if your five-year business plan projects a total of twenty-five, you will need to make sure that your EHR system can grow along with your practice.

- As more EHR vendors come online, competition for business becomes more acute and many vendors are offering incentives—additional services and even financial rewards—to doctors who choose their systems. Do not allow the incentives to sway your decision. The system has to be right for you and your practice. Investigate the vendor as you investigate their system. Does their track record suggest that they will be around to provide service in three or four years?
- Ask about security. Patient authentication, HIPAA-compliant communications, and encryption for email transmissions are all essential.
- Plan for phased-in implementation. Your EHR decision may be partially driven by your budget, but it will also be affected by the state of the technology. As EHR is more widely adopted and standards of practice are established, the software has to catch up. By implementing your system in phases, you may be able to take advantage of improved software when your practice is ready for it.
- Plan for the implementation and learning curve. Doctors and staff need to make a commitment to use the new system and invest time in hands-on training. At the same time, the information from paper health records must be entered into the system and double-checked for accuracy. These steps are almost certain to temporarily reduce office efficiency. Ask your vendor about on-site training.
- Plan for maintenance costs. You may be handy with your personal computer, but you should not rely on your own skills for EHR system support. The costs, duration, and nature of specific services covered in the maintenance contract should be spelled out clearly.

- Make proofreading and double-checking a part of your office protocol. Just as illegible handwriting can cause medical errors, a wrong keystroke can have far-reaching effects. Users of EHR—doctors and staff—should always review their own work for accuracy, but then files must be double-checked by someone else and finally by the doctor.
- As you are selecting your system, think *intuitive, simple, work flow,* and *security.* You may be tempted by the bells and whistles, but it is the day-to-day, easy, efficient, time- and cost-saving system that will prove most satisfactory for you and your staff over the long haul.
- Your system should be easily accessible from your home or traveling work station as well as from your office.
- Some systems offer *call center* services that allow facilitated off-site care and patient and physician communication through an operator. The abilities of such call centers go far beyond the usual answering service.

As you, your colleagues, and your patients become more comfortable with EHR, and EHR protocols are further streamlined, consider the opportunities for revenue building. Services such as online consultations and patient connectivity may have financial benefits, either through insurance reimbursement or direct payment.

Your decision to implement EHR technology will have significant initial costs in terms of money, time, and productivity. However, the promise of greater accuracy, information access, increased revenue, and significantly improved patient care will repay your investment for years to come. If you take the time to consider your purchase carefully and commit yourself to integrating technology into your practice, you will soon be wondering how you ever practiced medicine without Electronic Health Records.

# Computer Discussion and Planning Checklist

❏ PC vs. Mac
❏ Desktop and laptop integration
❏ Docking stations
❏ Essential system components—processor, clock rate, RAM, hard drive
❏ Monitors
❏ Scanners
❏ Projectors
❏ Handheld devices
❏ Backup power source
❏ Firewall
❏ DVD/CD burner
❏ USB ports
❏ Electronic Health Record systems
❏ Practice management software
❏ HL7 protocols (standards of health care information)
❏ Word processing software
❏ Time and billing software
❏ Accounting software
❏ Virus protection software, including anti-spam, anti-spyware, and anti-adware
❏ Tape backup software or other data backup system
❏ Spreadsheet software
❏ Practice-specific software
❏ Presentation software
❏ Media player
❏ Adobe Acrobat
❏ Computer training
❏ Computer maintenance and technical support
❏ Upgrading

# chapter six:
# Personnel

Once you have chosen your office space, it is time to decide how the clerical, administrative, and nursing work is going to be done for your practice. Before even thinking about hiring your first employee, you must keep in mind that all personnel are entitled to certain legal rights, and you should know what those legal rights are. Generally, a sense of fairness and sensitivity will help you avoid personnel problems. Nevertheless, there are certain legal responsibilities that an employer must observe, and you should be aware of them when you start your practice. Some of the main legal requirements fall into two main categories: civil rights, and work safety and fairness.

## CIVIL RIGHTS

There are several key civil rights acts that every employer must be aware of.

- *Civil Rights Act of 1964.* This act makes it unlawful for employers with fifteen or more employees to discriminate against people based on race, color, religion, national origin, or sex with regard to hiring and employment.

- *Age Discrimination and Employment Act of 1967.* This Act prohibits firms with twenty or more employees from discriminating against workers forty years of age or over.
- *Rehabilitation Act of 1973.* This Act prohibits discrimination against physically or mentally disabled people in federal contracts.
- *Pregnancy Discrimination Act of 1978.* This Act requires that pregnancy be treated as any other medical condition.
- *Immigration Reform and Control Act of 1986.* Employers must verify proof of citizenship and legal residency of their employees in the United States. Each employer must keep a completed federal I-9 form for each employee hired after 1986.
- *Americans with Disabilities Act of 1990.* This Act prohibits employers of fifteen or more employees from discriminating against people with disabilities, and requires that employers provide them with accommodations that do not pose an undue hardship.
- *Older Workers Benefit Protection Act of 1990.* This Act prohibits discrimination with respect to employee benefits based on age and regulates early retirement benefits.

## WORK SAFETY AND FAIRNESS

There are also several work safety and fairness acts an employer should be aware of.

- *Occupational Safety and Health Act of 1970* (OSHA). Employers must provide safe working conditions for workers. In addition to this requirement is the *Hazard Communication Standard*, which is a means of informing employees about hazards and how to respond to them.
- *Employee Polygraph Protection Act of 1988.* This Act makes it unlawful for employers to request lie detector tests from employees or job applicants.

- Workers' compensation laws. These are laws on the books of the various states, and their requirements and benefits vary. Check your state laws with the help of your insurance broker and your accountant.
- *Employee Retirement Income Security Act of 1974* (ERISA). This Act governs operations of pensions and retirement benefits provided by private employers. If you have joined a retirement trust plan for employees, this Act may affect you. The employee trust program is a way for small enterprises to give employees benefits by joining a larger group. Check with your insurance broker to see if any of these requirements apply to you.
- Posting notices in a prominent location. This usually is done in the employee lounge—or if you do not have a lounge, near the coffee maker or water cooler—so that there is no doubt that the employees have an opportunity to see all of the required postings. Check with your insurance broker and your accountant to determine which notices are required.

# MEDICAL OFFICE PERSONNEL

You, your colleagues, and your staff set the tone and mood of your office, which your patients detect immediately. The team approach with valued staff is crucial for your business success as a medical practice.

Doctors often come to the practice through personal contact, referral, an association listing, or by invitation from the doctors already in practice. Doctors may be obtained through medical newspaper advertisements as well, particularly when the practice is looking for a specialist. The use of professional placement services or headhunters may not be cost-effective in the beginning of your practice, but it is worthwhile for you to check into their cost, especially if you find that you are having difficulties getting job applicants.

Skilled medical personnel, especially nurses, are worth their weight in gold and may be obtained through advertisements, and by referral. Be sure to check with your colleagues at local hospitals, as they may know of talented people looking for private practice positions. Agencies and staffing companies are good sources as well.

Physicians are realizing the importance of excellent patient care by incorporating the use of ancillary personnel in their practice. Nurse practitioners, physicians' assistants, and others with special skills practicing under supervision and protocols are in great demand today. (When building your staff, you may need nurse practitioners to give better care to your patients.) Having an experienced and competent office manager is also critical for your success.

As you are reviewing applications and interviewing front office clerks, back office support nurses, and other associates, make sure they have good references, good work habits, and good skills. In large metropolitan areas, temporary employment agencies can fill these positions for you on a part-time or short-term, full-time basis, so you do not need to hire someone full-time. However, if you employ someone through an employment agency, this may add a great deal of expense to your staff costs. The agency collects a fee on part-time workers and is entitled to a fee from you if you hire the person it recommends.

One of the most rewarding ways to obtain seasoned personnel is through organizations that specialize in the employment of people who have retired or who are over 40. People with considerable and valuable experience as secretaries or assistants add value to your medical practice, and they can save you time and give you practical advice.

If the partnership or group of doctors exceeds three or four, it is advisable to hire an *office administrator*. This person typically has extensive experience in medical office administration. A practice of ten to fifteen doctors will need professional, outside consulting for some management issues. A medical practice of fifteen or more doctors must have highly trained medical office management.

You may decide to use a secretarial service where a secretary can come to your office on one or more days a week and do the filing, typing, and other office functions that are necessary. Such contract workers do not require withholding accounts as do regular employees.

Such options give the beginning medical practice a lot of flexibility and means of expanding its impact without having the burden of maintaining full-time personnel when capital is limited. Additionally, you only use them when you need them and you do not have a lot of downtime for your employees when the workload is erratic, as it may be when you are starting your practice.

If you are sharing office space, you may also want to share the talents and costs of secretaries, administrative staff, nurse practitioners, physicians' assistants, and advanced practice nurses. The type of nursing support personnel when you start your practice not only depends on the specialty but your patient load. Your own professional judgment is critical on this subject. An important resource is your professional association and academics especially in medical management. Inquire of your colleagues in your specialty for suggestions.

## Nurse Practitioners

*Nurse practitioners* (NPs) are registered nurses who complete advanced education and training, often leading to graduate degrees. Nurse practitioners became an important part of the health care system in the mid-1960s because of a national shortage of physicians. The initial programs were in pediatrics, but soon included many other specialties.

Nurse Practitioners take health histories, perform complete physical exams, diagnose, and test many common acute or chronic problems. They interpret laboratory results and X-rays, prescribe and manage medications and therapies, provide supportive counseling and health teaching, and refer patients to other health professionals. They emphasize health maintenance and prevention of illness.

In the United States, NPs generally have prescription privileges, but levels and privileges vary from state to state, and you should become familiar with the practice requirements and privileges in your practice jurisdiction. As of 2006, there are approximately 145,000 NPs nationwide.

Although NPs practice extensively in institutions (such as hospitals, long-term care facilities, correctional institutions, schools, and colleges), they also are valuable in private practices. They provide cost-effective, high-quality care.

## Physicians' Assistants

*Physicians' assistants* (PAs) perform some similar functions as NPs, but unlike NPs, they may not work independently or in collaboration with a physician, but are instead licensed to work under the supervision of a physician.

Physicians' assistants train in accredited programs, and upon graduation, they take a national certification examination. If they are successful, they are eligible for a state license. Although NPs and PAs may work together, PAs must be supervised by a physician.

To learn more about the scope of education and responsibilities of PAs and NPs, go to the websites for the Academy of Physicians' Assistants at **www.aapa.org** and the American College of Nurse Practitioners at **www.acnpweb.org**.

## Advanced Practice Nurses

The term *advanced practice nurse* is descriptive of several health care providers, such as NPs, certified nurse midwives (CNM), clinical nurse specialists (CNS), and certified registered nurse anesthetists (CRNA).

They all make independent and collaborative health care decisions. They are clinicians demonstrating leadership as administrators, researchers, consultants, and educators.

# WHO TO HIRE

Before selecting any staff, review in your mind the qualities you are seeking in the people that you hire. Naturally, everyone wants pleasant, cooperative, and happy people around when running a medical office. Rarely can you tell from an interview whether people are going to fulfill these expectations. Their résumés and work history, including references, can give you a good idea as to the quality of their work. You should talk to those personal reference contacts as a way to determine their work habits and behavior in the office relating to others, especially patients.

When you are beginning your medical practice, two functions are crucial and are best performed by two different people. The first is the *bookkeeping* function. An accountant familiar with the practice of medicine should be hired immediately. The accountant can either perform the bookkeeping function for you or recommend a bookkeeper to you. It can be helpful when the bookkeeper and the accountant have worked together in the past and know how to work efficiently with each other.

It is important to find a bookkeeper who will give you continuity over a long period of time, because you will need bookkeeping and accounting information for taxes and other business reporting purposes. You want someone in that position who loves to do detail work. If you only have one staff person to be assistant, receptionist, and bookkeeper, you may want to outsource the bookkeeping function until you can afford to hire an in-house bookkeeper.

The second essential position is *office manager*. Quite often, the first full-time employee that you will hire is an office manager. The manager will sometimes do double duty in the front office, so you want to look for the gregarious, outgoing type of person who will give your practice a pleasant image in the minds of others. An experienced office manager can be a valuable asset to your practice. Not only can they do more work because they are experienced, but they can also give you good advice. As you acquire additional staff, such as nurses, certified medical assistants, or nurse practitioners, the office manager will handle the work flow and more experienced employees can mentor newer employees as they join the practice. An experienced office manager can also handle routine interviewing of new hires, performance evaluations, and termination of employment.

There are numerous considerations in the management needs of the practice, and three of the most important are the number of staff to oversee, whether the practice is in a growth mode or developed and stable mode, and the physicians' role in leadership. Some physicians do not want to be involved in leadership and leave that to others. Frequently, the office manager assumes the role, and the choice of such a manager becomes extremely critical in that circumstance.

Successful medical practices require both management and leadership. The criteria for both are different. Managers are good at keeping the status quo and adding stability and order to the office. Leaders tend to be good at inspiring people's expectations and taking the organization into a new direction. Leaders can appear to be difficult to get along with because they have a vision of where the organization should go. Managers are easier to deal with because they are more interested in keeping things functioning as usual.

Whether you call the office manager a practice manager or practice administrator, the title makes no difference. The role varies with the nature of the practice. One mistake that physicians make is hiring an office manager, practice manager, or office administrator who is unable to grow with the practice as it moves from a small practice into a larger one.

Good office managers combine the qualities of leadership and management. They can maintain the strengths of the organization and lead it into positive, new directions.

The most common causes of the failure of an office manager are when either the wrong person was hired for the job, or once the right person was hired, that person's ability to do the job was impeded by the physicians or by staff. A good manager is the office hub. With a skilled manager in place, your organization functions very well and everyone prospers.

Human resources (HR) issues are now so complex and involved with statutory regulations that small practices often turn them over to outside consultants, while large practices are more likely to hire a full-time, in-house HR manager. Since the advent of health insurance as the backbone of financing medical treatment, coding has become extremely important, and in small, beginning practices this is a critical function. Only experienced clerks and managers should be given the responsibility of such important duties.

## THE INTERVIEW

Nothing substitutes for the personal interview. You want to hire someone who is pleasant, articulate, and who dresses neatly and shows signs of having good personal habits, which can relate directly to work habits. You should require at least three references from past employers. Other types of personal references (such as friends, ministers, and teachers) are fine, but employment references are essential and must be followed up. You can learn a great deal about the person during a very pleasant conversation with someone who is giving a reference. If the candidate has limited employment experience, you should get a personal reference from each prior employer.

When you call to discuss the applicant, you should keep your manner as pleasant and as positive as possible. If the prior employment experience was pleasant, you will probably get a happy narration of positive attributes. If the employment situation was not positive, you will have difficulty getting any information from a prior employer. Consider carefully before you hire someone who had a bad experience with a prior employer. Such bad experiences happen all the time and no one can be faulted for having them. Nevertheless, if a person has a pattern of personality differences with employers, you should consider that a red flag and be cautious.

Since the office manager is, at least initially, going to be doing the bulk of the clerical work on your behalf, you should have some idea of the proficiency of the applicant. This can be determined by standard tests that are given in secretarial schools so that you know how many words per minute the applicant can type, the percentage of accuracy, what software and computer systems the applicant has proficiency in, and at what levels. A person with realistic expectations when applying for such a job as an office manager should make his or her technical proficiency available to you without any trouble. Anyone who is reluctant for you to learn how proficient their error-free typing is should be given a very low consideration for hiring.

Regardless of the position for which the interview is conducted, here are some suggested, general interview questions:

- Why did you leave your last place of employment?
- If you come with us, what are your salary expectations?
- What are your goals within your profession?
- What kind of professional education, if any, are you planning on pursuing?
- Five years from now, where would you like to be in your profession?

Always trust your intuitive feelings about people, especially when you are interviewing them.

# POLICIES AND PROCEDURES

As soon as you start making decisions about your practice's policies and procedures—and that should be early in the planning stages—begin creating manuals. They will grow along with your practice. *Policies and procedures manuals* promote the efficient operation of your office and enable new and temporary employees to function in the office with a minimum of explanation. Every employee should get copies of your manuals and be notified of periodic updates.

Easily updated electronic manuals can be supplemented with samples of forms and other materials kept in a binder. One staff person, usually an office administrator, should be responsible for keeping the manuals current.

## Policy Manual Checklist

❏ Confidentiality
❏ Attendance at meetings
❏ Respect for all persons
❏ Harassment issues
❏ Smoking
❏ Dress code and grooming
❏ Conduct and decorum
❏ Housekeeping
❏ Holiday observances
❏ Lines of authority

## Procedures Manual Checklist

**NOTE:** *Include explicit, step-by-step guidelines for each task in the office.*

Human resources issues:
❏ Office hours
❏ Appointments, vacation, sick leave, and other time-off issues
❏ Overtime
❏ Leave of absence, such as maternity or paternity
❏ Bereavement
❏ Grievances, ombudsman, etc.
❏ Resignation, suspension, termination
❏ Harassment
❏ Working from home
❏ Job sharing
❏ Part-time employment

❑ Health insurance
❑ Time sheets, pay periods, other payroll issues
❑ Profit-sharing
❑ Bonuses
❑ Training opportunities

Other procedural issues:
❑ Indexing protocols for paper and electronic files
❑ Detailed description of new patient protocols
❑ Computer log-ons
❑ Procedures for file backup
❑ Phone system
❑ Mail system, messengers, express services, logging deliveries
❑ Other equipment (photocopiers, printers, scanners, postage meters, etc.)
❑ Accounting, accounts payable, reimbursements, petty cash
❑ System for reviewing and filing practice-related business contracts
❑ List and sample of all forms used in the office with current revision date
❑ Staff roster
❑ Frequently used numbers and emergency contact information, including hospitals, pharmacies, medical consultants, medical association, temporary agencies, messenger services, contract services, computer technician, landlord, plumber, etc.
❑ Safety issues, including disposal of sharps, use of gloves, sterilization, etc.
❑ Emergency procedures, including location of first aid kit and Automatic Electronic Defibrillator (AED), CPR/AED instructions, and evacuation plan with map
❑ Federal and local government required postings for employees to view

# chapter seven:
# Outside Support Services

Your medical practice will benefit from a professional relationship with a certified public accountant (CPA), a reliable insurance broker, a real estate agent, and a variety of other consultants.

As has been said earlier, a real estate agent is mandatory while looking for office space, particularly if you are going to be leasing. You should choose someone who is familiar with the geographical area, who has a reputation for being trustworthy, and whom you personally like. Look for a commercial real estate agent who has experience with medical practices, since he or she may have access to information about space in medical office buildings or practices that are closing or moving.

Choosing an accountant is extremely important, because your medical practice will function smoothly only if income, expenses, and other financial transactions are provided for in an orderly fashion. A set of books must be established for you, and there are accounting needs that will apply uniquely to the practice of medicine.

An insurance broker is also a necessity in setting up a medical practice, and remember to keep nurturing your relationship with your bankers, because they can keep you informed of financial programs that are constantly being developed by lending institutions.

## FINDING TRUSTWORTHY CONSULTANTS

Today's medical practices require more than knowledge of medicine—they require solid business, accounting, and financial acumen as well. Even doctors who have excellent skills in these other areas find that there is not enough time to be doctor, decision-maker, and administrator. Many doctors select management or financial consultants to help coordinate those levels of practice.

Experts and consultants may advertise in medical journals and newspapers, but word of mouth is often the best way to locate trustworthy experts. As you talk with other doctors, you can ask for their recommendations for accountants, computer experts, and even interior designers. Regardless of where you get a referral, always check references.

Look for advisors with whom you feel comfortable and who have the appropriate credentials and experience. Your initial meeting with such consultants is usually free. Take the time to discuss work styles, long-range goals, and problems you anticipate or already have with your practice. Ask about the consultant's experience working with other physicians in similar practice situations and be sure there are no conflicts of interest. Fee arrangements may vary, depending on the time commitment involved. In some cases, a monthly retainer is best, while in others, a flat fee or even an hourly consultant fee will work best. Ask the consultant for a written proposal. Check references carefully. When you have reached an agreement, draw up a contract that states very explicitly what you have agreed upon:

what work the consultant will do, for how long, where, and for what fee. Include a statement explaining how either party can terminate the relationship.

Geographic proximity may be desirable in working with any of those professionals mentioned. You many want to have meetings and conferences in your office or their office.

Once you have hired the consultant, go over your philosophy, ethics, values, goals, dreams, and other details about the business. Discuss finances and financial planning, taxes, audits, insurances, benefit packages, growth, goals, retirement plans, and all that is on your mind for the success of your practice.

# BUSINESS MANAGERS

A medical business manager focuses on your goals and the impact of business decisions, and helps keep your practice on track. While they are not directly involved with the day-to-day administration of your practice, business managers may be able to advise you on many of the day-to-day choices you have to make, including hiring, financing, expanding, or adding another doctor to your practice. They will need to be certified to work in a number of areas and to troubleshoot when problems arise. Some of their responsibilities may include:

- writing a business plan to reflect your attitudes and values;
- keeping current on your financial data, net worth, and profits;
- identifying goals and objectives that benefit the practice; and,
- anticipating problems that may interfere with the practice's goals.

# ACCOUNTANTS

Before opening your doors, you should obtain the services of a good accountant who has experience in dealing with medical practices. The accountant will be entrusted to set up your accounting system, your ledgers for each bank account, the accounting system for billing for each file, and the systems for payroll deductions.

There are many accounting systems to choose from, and the accountant you engage will explain the value and unique features of the ones you should consider. An accountant who has experience with medical practices will be an excellent advisor and help you make sound financial decisions. If you are implementing Electronic Health Records, it will be essential that your accountant is conversant with the system, since billing, insurance, and other financial transactions are handled through EHR.

Banks will be very accommodating as you set up your practice. They will have materials on how accounts should be monitored, and will help you and your accountant deal with this aspect of the practice. Additionally, banks can provide payroll withholding services for you, at a fee, and your accountant may urge you to avail yourself of that service. Your entire payroll can be handled by the bank, which relieves you and your accountant of a very cumbersome and expensive process. Your bank may do your payroll for you at little or no charge if you keep all of your deposits and loans with it.

Your accountant should make certain that you obtain the necessary SS-4 and SS-8 forms, which are the *Application for Employer Identification Number* and *Determination of Employee Work Status for Purposes of Federal Employment Taxes Income Tax Withholding*, respectively. These and the following should be discussed with your accountant:

- obtaining a tax ID number;
- setting up a payroll process (with a bank or other service);
- furnishing monthly profit and loss statements;
- providing accounts receivable and accounts payable figures as needed, no less than quarterly; and,
- setting up special accounts for taxes, such as FICA, Social Security, Medicare, and quarterly payment schedules.

# BANKS

Having a banker working with you is essential in starting up any business, particularly a professional medical practice. First, you want to establish a connection with a bank and develop a credit rating. One of the ways to do this is to borrow a small amount of money from the bank and pay it back promptly. You can speak candidly with your banker on how to do this.

Borrowing the money needed to start and run your medical practice is almost a necessity. You will need money for insurance, payroll funds, facility improvements, equipment purchases, lease fees, and a variety of other expenses. Patients do not always pay their bills on time, and you need flexibility in your cash flow to cover necessities.

The banker can really help a new business and help keep established businesses running. A banker can help with issues of debt management as well as other financial matters. A few of the things that you should discuss with your banker on a regular basis include the following:

- your written financial statement after obtaining it from your accountant;
- establishing a line of credit so that you can obtain funds quickly;

- the costs, if any, of having the bank provide you with your employee withholding and payroll services;
- the process of obtaining an ATM card; and,
- the possibility of consolidating consumer loans, such as credit card or car payment loans, and even student loans. Some banks offer consolidation plans that may be favorable for you.

# INSURANCE

Obtaining the services of a reliable insurance broker is crucial, not only to help you understand and obtain coverage, but also to help control the cost of various types of policies you will need. Finding someone who truly has your interests at heart and your needs in mind may not be easy. Talk to a few different agents and compare the information you receive about your insurance needs. A good broker knows that as you and your practice grow, your insurance needs develop, and more business flows to the broker. If that broker has treated you fairly and professionally, a relationship can last a long time and be mutually beneficial.

Insurance is available to cover nearly any event. However, being protected for anything and everything comes at a steep price. When making your insurance decisions, you must weigh the risks involved against the likelihood of the event. In every area there are disasters, such as hurricanes, floods, fires, civil disturbances, earthquakes, labor strikes, or other events that can have a catastrophic impact on your staff and your practice. When disasters occur, their effects may last for a long time.

Consider which disasters are most likely in your area and consider insurance coverage to provide for these emergencies. Flood insurance, earthquake insurance, and hurricane insurance can be extremely expensive and you may not be able to afford this kind of coverage. Your business interruption policy may not cover these emergencies, so this is an important part of your discussion with your insurance broker. Know where you are protected and where you are not. The welfare of your staff comes first, and you should create a written emergency plan to protect office personnel, again, taking into account the disasters that are most likely in your geographical region.

The beginning medical practice must have various forms of insurance coverage in place when the doors open. If the practice has full-time employees, or part-time employees who work a certain number of hours, depending on the jurisdiction, *workers' compensation* is required.

*Professional liability*, also known as malpractice insurance, is not only desirable, but in some jurisdictions, mandatory. In the practice of medicine, it is absolutely necessary. Just as in the legal profession, changes are occurring in the public's willingness to sue doctors. Both professions have become targets for lawsuits from disgruntled patients or clients, and insurance coverage protection is costly, but necessary.

This shift has also caused a change in the way coverage is triggered. Today most malpractice insurance is what has come to be called *claims-made*. This is coverage that is triggered by the making of a claim against the doctor by someone and reported to the company during the policy period. This is contrasted with the older form of *occurrence* coverage, which is no longer in use, where the date of the occurrence triggered coverage.

Because of the nature of claims-made coverage, you should have insurance that covers you even after your medical practice has terminated. This is sometimes called *tail coverage*, and your broker can explain it in better detail.

In choosing your medical malpractice insurance, check with your colleagues, associations, hospital administrators, as well as with the *Physicians Insurers Association of America* (PIAA), which is a group of physician-owned and -operated companies that provide more than 60% of the medical malpractice coverage in the United States and other countries.

Companies in the PIAA can access important ongoing research, valuable current education programs, and excellent networking resources. They also support meaningful medical liability reform in the United States, to better serve doctors, dentists, hospitals, and other health care professionals.

The American Medical Association section on Medical Office Management can be extremely helpful in giving you sources to find which kind of malpractice insurance is best for you. There are also policies provided by the medical associations in many areas, and these should be examined carefully. They can be very helpful and can be quite economical, compared to insurance in the open market. There may be some group insurance benefits through the medical association, and the association may have policies that include coverage that will make the package economical for you.

Premises liability insurance is extremely important, as is automobile liability insurance. It protects you from liability when you or your staff members drive a vehicle in the course of employment.

With all of these liability areas covered, you can next consider the expense of other types of insurance that are not critical at the moment you open your doors, but become more and more critical as you develop your practice. Health, life, and disability insurance are in this category, along with accidental death and dismemberment coverage.

Other options include *business-related insurance*, such as a keyman life or disability policy that will provide for the overhead if the important doctor in the practice becomes disabled or dies. In the business insurance policy that covers you for property damage, there should be a provision for business interruption insurance, and you should have document replacement insurance.

You would also be well advised to include coverage for *employment practices liability*. This covers liability for suits brought by employees for sexual harassment and wrongful termination, for example. There are even relatively new policies for liability associated with your website, your advertising, and things of that nature.

The *fidelity bond*, which you should obtain for any employee handling money, is a vital part of your insurance package. An important element of protection from an insurance point of view is the umbrella policy of excess coverage protection that can be available over and above your personal liability, vehicle liability, and premises liability coverage.

With the need to make and balance so many choices, it is extremely important that you obtain the services of a reputable insurance broker who can guide you into the kinds of coverage you need. You may have to obtain a special broker to acquire professional liability coverage.

Review the costs of insurance very carefully, and weigh just as carefully the need for certain kinds of insurance and the insurance face amounts. Discuss your needs in detail with your insurance broker and make your insurance decisions based on those discussions.

Special note should be made about the insurance crisis in many states. As a result of large verdicts and increasing premiums, some states have attempted to cap noneconomic damages, such as pain and suffering and emotional distress, which account for approximately 60% of large awards. California has such a cap at $250,000 and its constitutionality has been upheld by its courts. Other states have not found such constitutionality. There has been a serious attempt at the federal level to have Congress enact such caps, but this has not been established at the time of this writing. You should inquire of your professional liability carrier of the status of MICRA in your state. This cap legislation is called the *Medical Injury Compensation Reform Act* (MICRA). It has been the model for reforms in Colorado, Florida, Indiana, Montana, Texas, and Virginia. It works because insurance premiums are reduced and medical benefits are available to many more people. In addition, there has been an attempt in some states to legislate a no-fault system resembling workers' compensation.

---

### Insurance Checklist

❏ Comprehensive general liability insurance
❏ Professional liability insurance
❏ Premises liability insurance
❏ Workers' compensation insurance
❏ Business interruption insurance
❏ Disability insurance
❏ Office overhead insurance
❏ Medical Injury Compensation Reform Act (MICRA) effective in your state or not

---

# chapter eight:
# Your Medical Library

Many valuable library materials are available online, on DVDs, and on other electronic media. While shelves of books may be unnecessary for medical research purposes, a small office library can provide rapid access to resources that can be used in your work, your writing, and your conversations with patients.

Depending on the number of volumes in your library and the size and layout of your office space, your library could be housed along one wall of a hallway, in a conference room, or on the walls of your office. Having your important books close at hand makes access to the volumes easier. As a bonus, books also help with soundproofing.

Building a traditional, printed medical library is less important when your office is near a medical school library or a hospital library. Nevertheless, it makes sense to have the latest volumes available for research and information, particularly in your practice specialty.

As you develop your practice, it may become clear that a print library is not desirable or practical. Unless you happen to collect antique medical books, a medical library is effective only if it is current. Printed libraries can be very expensive. Keeping supplements current and adding new volumes as the need arises becomes a large part of the expense of maintaining a library. Office libraries are capital investments and can be depreciated. Your tax advisor can be helpful as you make decisions about such purchases.

# GETTING BOOKS

If you are a recent medical school graduate, you may receive offers for special discounts and other deals in the purchase of books from medical book publishers. These are very attractive, and most of them are exceedingly worthwhile. However, you should balance your ability to pay with your desire for certain sets of volumes. A judicious selection of books coupled with the publishers' discounts can make a big difference in the expenses of your practice.

The purchase of used books can reduce your library costs. When libraries are being broken up, such as when a practice is closing, books will often become available at attractive prices. Also, when practices merge, duplicate volumes may be sold. Medical libraries at hospitals or medical schools may also sell duplicate or slightly damaged copies of books.

For all doctors, beginning or otherwise, it is helpful to have a working relationship with a major medical book publisher's representative who calls on you either in person, or by phone or email to keep track of your needs. It is important to establish this relationship rather quickly. These representatives can be valuable sources of information on the location of libraries that are being broken up. You will be able to take advantage of book bargains much more rapidly by dealing with the people who are closest to the book market.

# THE ELECTRONIC MEDICAL LIBRARY

Electronic research data is increasingly vital to the practice of medicine. Medical schools and large practices have research resources, including legal resources such as LexisNexis, and they can be made available to a beginning practitioner through their facility. Medical schools provide training in the operation of these services, and the services themselves provide training for the use of their systems. Computer-based services are helpful in finding out about drug trials, treatment results, journal articles, and specialized or supplemental research to make certain that you are using the latest information in your work. These services are not free, and the cost for their usage can be substantial. A beginning practitioner may wish to contact local medical libraries regarding their policies on the use of computer terminals and the fees for their services. In an office-sharing arrangement, shared online services may be available and included in the rental cost, or may be billed separately.

CD-ROM technology is not only replacing books, but is also making vast amounts of research material available to small offices and sole practitioners in a minimum amount of space. Entire libraries can be on CD-ROM, and the necessary updates, supplements, and access can be managed electronically and quite simply. More importantly, in areas where square foot rental costs are problematic, these entire libraries can be maintained in a very small space.

# ESSENTIAL MEDICAL LIBRARY STARTERS

Your local medical librarian and hospital librarian can be very helpful in assisting you in making a list of essential print and electronic library materials. The resources from the American Medical Association and your local medical association sections pertaining to office management can also assist with this process.

Fundamental publications—such as medical digests, summaries, and dictionaries—will form the heart of your beginning selections. As you get into your practice, you will modify the following list, but it does provide a starting point for your medical library.

---

### Medical Library Checklist

❏  Medical dictionary
❏  Directory of local doctors
❏  Standard English dictionary
❏  Basic instructions and handouts for patients
❏  General texts in your area of expertise
❏  Medical specialty texts
❏  Physicians' Desk Reference
❏  An illustrated anatomy text
❏  Code books (including Current Procedural Terminology and International Classification of Disease)

---

# chapter nine:
# Financing

To begin a medical practice, you must have enough money to fund the essentials for such an enterprise. Intuitively, this seems to be a catch-22 situation, because you have to have money to make money.

If this prospect brings on anxiety or depression, you are not alone—and the situation is not hopeless. One of the best ways to reduce anxiety in any situation is to face the subject head-on and examine the options that are available to you. Rarely is there a situation in which a person has absolutely no options. By examining them, solutions can be found, personal tension can be reduced, and a vital step in professional success can be made.

## RAISING CAPITAL

There are several ways of raising the capital necessary to start a medical practice. The first is by having money available through savings, gifts, or the sale of assets. Savings can come from the income of the partners, who are working in other positions, or from a married couple pooling their income to fund a share in a budding medical practice. Gifts can come from family, such as parents or grandparents, and the sale of assets can occur under any number of circumstances. Selling assets can be a problematic way of raising funds, because the assets may be earning income and the choice of having income reduced creates a new catch-22.

If you are willing to devote your practice time to charitable pro bono activities, you may want to explore the charitable foundations that make grants available to doctors who spend time on worthwhile causes that would not otherwise receive a doctor's attention. Keep in mind, however, that whenever you are involved in a government and the use of its money, or a grant and the use of its funds, you must be willing to tolerate the paperwork. Governments and charitable organizations must justify every penny that is spent, and since there is no profit involved, the only way the expenditure of the money can be traced and evaluated is through paperwork.

Beginning your practice with outside money is good if you can obtain your loan early in the process. That allows you to hold your personal savings and other personal financial resources in reserve for opportunities that must be acted upon immediately—such as the purchase of a piece of equipment.

This money can come from the personal credit of the sole practitioner and the family involved, or the potential partners or shareholders and their families. Banks will take a first or second mortgage on real property to provide funds for establishing a new medical practice. The Small Business Administration has a loan guarantee program and Direct Loan Programs, and these avenues should be explored if all of the traditional sources of financing are unavailable.

Another form of credit is accounts receivable. When doctors are creating a new medical practice, they may already have been in practice and have patients on a regular basis. This provides not only an attractive asset for a bank, but may provide a stream of income that can be the basis for a working capital loan.

# DEBT MANAGEMENT

If financing is the most important element in beginning the medical practice, then debt management is the most important factor in keeping the practice financially viable. Regardless of the source of the start-up money, you should accept the fact that over the years of a medical practice, it is going to be necessary to have a good credit rating and a line of credit. Debt and borrowing is a necessary part of any business, and especially a personal service business such as a medical practice. Before you begin the first steps toward acquiring financing, you should develop a relationship with a bank and one of the bank's officers who will act as your personal banker and will get to know you and even your family.

Keep a close, ongoing relationship with your personal banker. Meet regularly for lunch, either quarterly or on whatever schedule seems reasonable for you both. You will want your accountant to prepare financial statements for your banker on a regular basis if you have outstanding loans. They may be the subject of your meetings. Your banker may be able to suggest someone as a financial advisor, for the practice and for you personally.

Debt management is something that changes constantly because your accounts payable and accounts receivable change constantly. Ask your accountant or your bookkeeper to provide you with frequent profit and loss statements that include the accounts payable and receivable figures. You may even want a quick statement of just the accounts receivable and payable.

There are always going to be amounts that are uncollectible, and they generally form a predictable percentage of your accounts. If you keep track of that percentage and factor it into the total figure you have, you can make an educated estimate of how much potential income you have, as well as how much short-term debt you must pay.

Work closely with your accountant and your banker if you see that your debt is getting to a point where it is going to be a problem. Insolvency, bankruptcy, or other financial crises can be avoided if you pay attention to your debt management.

## *Dealing with Student Loans*

Many of today's medical school graduates start their careers with six-figure debt. Even with scholarships and grants, loan obligations can far exceed what a new doctor might hope to earn in annual salary. Unfortunately, compounding interest means that debt becomes more expensive as it lingers unpaid. Repayment periods stretch out over ten, twenty, or thirty years. What is more, outstanding student loans can interfere with your ability to secure the business loans necessary to establish your practice.

Most student loans allow a six-month grace period after graduation before repayment must begin. Some lenders will defer (but not forgive) payments for other reasons. Some institutions may forgive student loans for graduates who go into public service or have family emergencies that take them out of practice. However, the best plan is to assume that you *will* have to repay your loan, and establish a system to do so as soon as possible. Simply making the monthly payment that appears on your statement may not be the best approach to your indebtedness. Consider some of the variables that can affect the balance and options for meeting your obligation.

- **Interest rate.** While the principal balance ticks downward ever so slowly, the interest on that balance continues to compound. Depending upon current market conditions, switching from a variable rate to a fixed rate of interest may reduce the overall cost of your loan.

- **Loan consolidation.** You may be repaying several loans that were issued at several different rates of interest, and making multiple payments each month. Consolidating these loans may enable you to secure a lower interest rate, but always measure such monthly savings against the total repayment cost for the life of the loan, which may be extended to thirty years.

- **Begin paying before you graduate.** In some cases, students can consolidate their loans and begin repayment at lower student rates while they are still in school, saving substantially on the lifetime cost of borrowing.

- **Special payment plans.** You may be able to structure or restructure your loan so that your payments gradually increase or are specifically tied to your income.

- **Repay sooner rather than later.** The sooner you can repay your loans, the less they will cost you. For example, a $60,000 loan at 4% interest will cost approximately $73,000 if paid off in ten years, but more than $103,000 if paid off over thirty years.

- **Check for early payment penalties.** As you become more successful, you may find yourself with a large influx of cash. If your loan allows early payments without penalty, consider paying down a substantial portion of your loan in addition to your usual monthly payment. Even adding $50 to your payment each month can significantly reduce the cost of your loan.

- **Talk with your lender.** The lender has every reason to want you to fulfill your repayment obligations, since if you default on your loan, the lender loses money. If you find yourself in a bind, talk with your lender or loan servicer as soon as possible. Do not wait until the warning notices and phone calls start arriving. By showing your intent to pay, you may find the lender more willing to accommodate you with a temporary reprieve or a reduced payment amount. Such accommodations are known as *forbearance.*

- **Talk with your family.** Family members, because they have a personal interest in your success, may be willing to help you by paying off a portion or all of your outstanding loans and structuring a repayment schedule at a lower interest rate. Reducing your interest rate by a point, a half-point, or even a quarter-point, can save you thousands of dollars over the life of the loan. A family member may even be willing to defer repayment for several years to allow you to establish your practice and build your client base and income.

Some medical associations have what they call a Student Loan Consolidation Program. This enables anyone with more than a certain amount, usually $7,500, in outstanding federal student loans to reduce monthly loan payments and lock in at the lowest available interest rate. These programs can make available a *federal consolidation loan,* which is part of the group of loans available under the *Federal Family Education Loan* (FFEL) program as authorized by the federal government. The Federal Consolidation Loan program was established by Congress to help student borrowers manage the burden of student loan debts.

With such a loan, you can combine all or some of your outstanding loans into a single one, even if the loans are currently held by more than one lender and are of different types. Such consolidation allows a choice of flexible repayment terms and low fixed interest rates for the life of the loan. Not only do you save on the lower interest rate, but you can also save an additional six-tenths of a percent if you consolidate your loans within your grace period (a specified period after you graduate and before you begin repaying your loan). You may consolidate any of the loans listed below, but only if you are combining a loan with at least one other eligible loan.

- Federal Stafford Loans, unsubsidized and subsidized (including Guaranteed Student Loan, GSL)
- Direct Stafford Loans, unsubsidized and subsidized
- Federal Supplemental Loans for Students (formerly Auxiliary Loans to Assist Students and Student Plus Loans)
- Federal Perkins Loans (formerly National Defense/ National Direct Student Loans, NDSL)
- Health Professions Student Loans, including loans for Disadvantaged Students (HPSL)
- Federal Insured Student Loans (FISL)
- Federal PLUS (parent loans)
- Direct PLUS Loans
- Federal Consolidation Loans, unsubsidized and subsidized
- Direct Consolidation Loans, unsubsidized and subsidized
- Nursing Student Loans (NSL)

The federal government regulates how the fixed interest rate is determined on your consolidation loan. By extending your loan term and selecting a repayment plan, you may lower your monthly payments by as much as half. However, be aware that by extending the repayment time, you may be creating an increase in your financial obligation. There is no penalty for early repayment of your consolidated loan, so you may pay it off at any time or simply make higher payments when you are able to do so.

For information on loan consolidation, you should contact a loan counselor at your medical school, medical association, or other organization with which you may be dealing regarding student loans. You will undoubtedly be contacted by an assortment of lenders and loan servicers who are eager to help you manage your debt. Consult a trusted financial advisor before changing the way you deal with your student loans.

Your decisions and actions regarding your indebtedness can affect your practice for years. Do not default on your loans. Be sure to make payments on time. Keep thorough and accurate records of payments. If you meet or speak with your lender, loan servicer, or financial advisor about your debt, keep a record of the date, the name of the person you spoke with, and the topics covered in your discussion. (It is always a good idea to follow up such conversations with a letter that confirms any agreements or decisions that were made.) Let your lender know immediately if you move or change your bank account or contact information. The following contacts may prove valuable for you in arranging for payment or consolidation of your loans:

**AMA  Student Loan Consolidation Program**
866-737-2979
www.ama-studentloans.com

When you are starting your practice, your outstanding student loans may seem an insurmountable obstacle to success. By establishing a reasonable repayment program, developing and following a practical budget, and working steadily toward your personal and professional goals, you will soon find yourself able to repay your loans and make more profitable use of the money you work so hard to earn.

# BUDGET

When you begin your practice, it is nice to have enough money to provide the furniture, equipment, supplies, and staff expenses for six to eight months. This will give you a minimal amount of time to send out a billing and receive payments on accounts receivable. Of course, you also have personal expenses and costs to take care of in that same period of time, and provisions must be made for both business and personal needs.

One of the ways to minimize or even eliminate the stress of the unknown in startup costs is to begin a rough budget of your monthly needs, even using estimates, and multiply them by six or eight months. That will give you the amount of start-up money that you should be looking for. A few phone calls will give you the monthly estimates for rent, equipment leasing, furniture leasing, and contract services for staff or other essential services. Simple office supplies can be easily estimated and included in this rough budget. A total of these expenses will give you a realistic estimate of what you will need to begin. Suddenly the anxiety of the unknown is reduced because you now have rational parameters.

Your rough budget should be in two basic parts. The first part is the startup costs, which will occur only once, such as buying furniture. The second part of such a budget should contain expense items and income items. The income, of course, must be an estimate.

# CASH FLOW

Another important aspect of operating a small business is keeping cash flow as regular as possible. Maintaining a regular and predictable amount of money coming in and going out is key. There are natural ebbs and flows in a business cycle. Your office may be especially busy during flu season or particularly quiet during the holidays. A loan from a bank may be necessary to smooth out these peaks and valleys. Your financial advisor may be able to help you think up creative ways to handle cash flow issues that do not involve loans or letting bills stack up.

chapter ten:
# The Organized Office

Having a computerized office makes it imperative that you establish a system not only for calendaring, but for opening, indexing, and cross-indexing charts, as well as other pertinent information that you may need outside of a patient file. Setting up future calendar dates—such as follow-up appointment notices—for the file is also advisable.

As used in this book, the information attributable to each individual patient is called a *chart*, and other information for administrative and management categories in the office are called *files*. For example, a doctor can open a patient's chart and get a quick overview of the patient's medical history. A file that has information with regard to the laboratory equipment or photocopier can provide information that has relatively little value to any particular patient.

## INDEXING

In beginning an office network, an index protocol should be established immediately. All those with access to the network must follow the protocol so that documents of a recurring nature and documents that pertain to particular projects will be identified in files where all users of the system can retrieve them easily. For example, all charts can be stored in one drive on the computer and all non-patient-related office information stored in another. The protocol may require that each patient is to be given a patient number or another form of code. The number can be created beginning with the year of the first entry along with the patent's initials, and then a number in sequence within the total patients at the time of the addition. This way, there can be no question as to when the patient came into the practice.

The filing of charts can then be done by the patient's initials with the numerical sequence and then the year the patient entered the practice in order for the protocol to have another emphasis, the patient's name or initials. The protocol for establishing a filing system can be done in many different ways, and there are commercial systems that solve these problems for you and create a lot of simple ways to save you time and money.

Administrative documents should be filed by major categories and subdirectories. For example, documents related to office administration could go in a subdirectory entitled "Administration" or "Office," and practice guides, such as sample memoranda or research sources, can go in a separate subdirectory. Job descriptions for personnel in your practice and their protocols should be in a separate subdirectory as well.

The key to effective storage and retrieval of documents is uniformity in naming the files. If a particular system user has a favorite method of identifying documents that is not readily apparent to other users, the document may be lost to other system users. File identification standards should be established immediately as part of the index protocol, at the outset of your practice.

# SETTING UP THE CHARTS AND FILES

The first document to go into the new chart or file is the general information pertaining to the subject. For a patient, it should contain all of the essential information necessary to maintain contact with the patient, such as name, address, home telephone and cell number, email addresses, emergency numbers, next of kin or other emergency contact, and the health insurance provider's name, policy number, group number, or any other pertinent information of the source of payment for the medical services. This way, communication may be maintained with the patient and with the insurer very easily.

After the chart has been opened and entered into the system, additional entries to the chart are made as the patient is progressing through examinations and treatment. This source of information is not only there to refresh your memory, but to guide others who take care of the patient if you are not in the office or are otherwise unavailable. The patient's interests are kept uppermost when all of the pertinent information is in the file. The chart should contain all details of examinations, treatments, prescriptions, hospitalizations, and test results. A record of the patient's appointments is also critical, including appointments that have been missed by the patient, which can be as critical as drug dosages.

Redundancy can be extremely valuable in maintaining files and charts. Damage to any part of the computer, particularly a hard drive and its data, would have disastrous effects not only on the practice but also on the patient. It is absolutely critical to have a backup system for computer data.

Safety is an important factor for your patients, and you want your patients to feel comfortable and trusting in their relationship with you and your office. The documentation that they are given at the beginning is critical to the atmosphere of trust that you want to create.

## OFFICE MANAGEMENT FORMS

Your practice management software will likely provide you with most of the forms you need, but there are additional form resources through medical associations, medical book stores, drug companies, and other sources. A complete set of forms and protocols for their use must be established before you open your doors to your first patient.

There are many standardized forms you will use, such as the patient intake form, which is filled out on the very first day before any treatment or examination is made. In addition to the patient information, it also important to include the identity of the person who made the referral to the physician. This not only helps you understand how patients are finding you, but lets you know who should be thanked.

A number of helpful forms are included here and throughout this book. They are suggestions for you to modify for your practice or to stimulate the creation of your own forms.

# Sample Symptom Diary*

Recording symptoms in a daily diary helps patients (and minor patients' parents) recognize precipitating stresses and patterns of reinforcement.

Date/day of week _____

Time started _____

Time stopped _____

Place _____

Activity_____

People present _____

_____

Symptom (describe)_____

_____

Location_____

_____

Description _____

_____

How bad? (1=mild, 5=medium, 10=worst possible) _____

_____

How long did it last? _____

_____

What did it keep you from doing? _____

_____

What brought it on?_____

_____

Thoughts _____

_____

Feelings _____

_____

Activities _____

_____

Food and time eaten _____

_____

What did you do?_____

_____

What made it better? _____

_____

What made it worse?_____

_____

What caused the symptom? _____

_____


* Adapted with permission from Barton D. Schmid, MD

# Patient Transfer Form
## [Letterhead]

_____

(address)

_____

_____

Re: (Patient)

Dear (Parent/Patient):

For quite some time, since ____(date)____, we have had the privilege of having you as our patient, and the time has come for you to move into another phase of your life.

You should continue to seek medical care and stay current with annual physicals and any other treatments that are necessary.

Please let us know if you would like a referral to a physician or to whom you would like us to forward your charts.

Thank you for our physician/patient relationship, and all of us wish you well in the future.

Very truly yours,

Dr. _____

## Missed Appointment Notice
[Letterhead]

_____
(address)

_____

_____
(phone number)

Re: _____

Dear _____:

Our records show that you missed an appointment to see us on _____. Please call us at the above number and make another appointment.

We look forward to seeing you soon.

Sincerely,

Dr. _____

## Referral Acknowledgment
[Letterhead]

_____
(address)

_____

_____

_____
(phone number)

Re: _____

Dear _____:

Thank you very much for referring the above patient to us for medical treatment. We will do our best to justify your confidence in us.

Sincerely,


Dr. _____

# ADMINISTRATION

Large practices and clinics often have nonphysician leadership and administration. Unless you are beginning your practice with that kind of structure, administration may be shared by a number of people. For example, a senior, founding physician may share administrative duties with an office manager.

When you begin a practice, various functions have to be fulfilled, and you as the physician may have to fulfill parts of several of them. That means you may have to study management and administrative techniques in order to fulfill that function. Human resources duties are also important because of the necessity to comply with employment requirements issued by state and federal governments, and by standards in the profession. Some functions, such as human resources and employment clearances, can be outsourced to agencies that specialize in those fields.

In larger clinics, these functions are given to a specific manager. However, in beginning a practice with one staff person or a small number of people starting out, you may have that responsibility as a shared part of administration.

There was a time when physicians could know just about all there was to know about running a medical practice as a business. That day has long passed, and physicians must be able to admit that they do not know many things about the business aspects of running a practice and should seek expert advice.

The *American College of Medical Practice Executives* (ACMPE) has brought forward a series of documents that define all of the important areas of knowledge and skills necessary for a person to be a successful administrator of a group medical practice. The information is valuable to medical practices of any kind. The ACMPE defines areas where the administrator must excel, including professionalism, leadership, and communication skills. Professional standards and technical knowledge and skills must be maintained. In leadership, the practice's strategic direction and organizational and analytical skills are supported. Communication skills require the presenting of information clearly and concisely to patients and to staff. Each of these traits must be developed if you are to be a physician participating in the administration of your practice.

Administration of the practice includes managerial functions. These can be defined generally as financial, marketing, risk, professional responsibility, information management, and the business and clinical operations. These categories give you an idea of the wide diversity of managerial functions that must be undertaken when a practice is established.

Research has shown that the better performing medical groups have excellent communication between physicians and administrative staff, good relationships with referring physicians, a professional attitude toward administration of colleagues and business, and a culture of respect in the practice, with an emphasis on quality care, good reputation, and patient satisfaction.

## Patient Flow

Regardless of the size of your practice, an organized and well managed *patient flow* system is the hallmark of a quality business. The process, which can be tracked as part of the patient's electronic record, can be divided into simple functions, such as registration, scheduling, arrival and check-in; management during the visit; and, the patient leaving with all of the important information being recorded before his or her departure.

The physical arrangement of the office is just as critical as the administrative functions. An established protocol defines how the patient is assigned and accompanied to an examination room, how the office staff indicates the order in which patients are to be seen, where the chart will be placed for the physician, and how special notes can be added to the chart by the office staff to alert the physician as to what the patient may have in mind. For example, a note about a patient's concern or complaint can be appended to the chart so that the physician can ask the patient about the problem.

## Risk Management

An additional management function includes the legal aspects of the practice, such as *risk management,* which minimizes the practice's risk of legal entanglement. Your discussions with your professional liability insurer or broker can be of great help in learning the basic aspects of risk management.

There are two categories of risk. The first is the risk of liability for the physical premises themselves to cause injury or death to people who come to the office. Second is the professional aspects of liability, which are covered in Chapter 14. A professional risk management consultant can advise you on how to minimize risks in your physical premises. This may be a cost item for you, but it will be well worth it in terms of reducing stress and financial exposure for liability, regardless of your insurance coverage. Consult with your insurer before you approve plans or commit to any investment in construction, changes, or tenant improvements in your prospective premises. If you are going to share space in a medical suite or a medical building that is part of a hospital, the management of those premises can be helpful in advising you how to minimize the risks that you may face in such an environment.

## Credentialing

A medical practice requires a great deal of documentation for the credentials of the physicians involved. A medical license is required in the jurisdiction where the practice is located, and in every jurisdiction where the physician may practice. When a physician joins the practice, such licensing must be carefully checked to make certain that there are no problems, such as suspensions, rejections, terminations, or any other things that may affect the license. To further complicate credentialing, managed-care companies, hospitals, insurance companies, state and federal regulators, and programs such as Medicare and Medicaid each require an application for provider status and maintenance of pertinent information on a prescribed schedule. This activity is different from state to state and from company to company.

Just keeping the credentialing in order and up to date can be a daunting task, depending upon the nature of the practice and the number of providers involved. The office administrator must make certain that information is available, stored, and maintained properly, including provider numbers for Medicare, Medicaid, state program, managed-care organizations, and insurance companies.

There are law firms that specialize in health care law, and you should utilize the services of one of those firms, particularly when you are starting your practice. As you progress, they will have an ongoing relationship with you and will be better able to serve you because of their familiarity with your practice.

## Contract Management

There are many contracts involved in the business side of the practice of medicine, including premises leases, equipment leases, employment agreements, laboratory agreements, waste disposal contracts, and others. Never assume that boilerplate contracts serve your best interests. Contracts must be read carefully and reviewed with legal counsel. Contracts are legal documents and should be filed in a consistent location, as established in your procedures manual.

You should be prepared to spend large sums of money on legal fees if you get embroiled in controversies involving contracts. However, contract controversies can often be dealt with quickly and inexpensively through negotiation or mediation.

## Billing and Collections

Aside from the high quality of the practice that you wish to maintain, the success of your billing and collections function is the next most critical to the success of the practice. The subject is addressed in detail in Chapter 11.

## Medical Records

The maintenance of patient medical records in the patient's chart is the primary function of the medical records unit. This unit may consist of a clerk or someone else in your practice who is trained and familiar with keeping medical records. These records must contain literally everything that pertains to the patient's personal information, treatment, examinations, and prognosis. There is a special emphasis on allergies, nurse's notes, self-care status, demographic information about the patient, laboratory and X-ray results, and orders.

The greatest problem of keeping medical records properly is keeping them complete. Information about the patient may come from many sources, such as hospitals, insurance companies, laboratories, specialists, other physicians, and even family members. This makes the patient's identification number and chart extremely important in centralizing the large amounts of detailed information on the patient.

Electronic Health Records (EHR) (see page 58) have had an enormous impact on patient recordkeeping. Still, whether you keep patient information electronically, in paper files, or a combination of the two, protocols for entering, checking, changing, and updating information must be established immediately and followed diligently. An error in a patient's chart—even a single character or digit—can create life-threatening problems, so training, accuracy, and double-checking are essential. Because electronic records do not have a physical presence—a file sitting on the desk as a reminder—protocols must also define how the doctor's orders for a patient will be followed. All of these decisions are part of the efficient administration of your practice.

## *Human Resources*

The function of human resources (HR) is responsible for administering all employment issues of the practice, including hiring, benefits, paid and unpaid time off, health insurance, pensions, taxes, promotions, raises, and employee termination. Human resources also establishes and implements policies for conduct in the office, and is responsible for developing the job descriptions of everyone involved in the practice as well as the protocols they must follow with respect to those tasks.

Other important aspects of human resources involve relationships between staff members, between patients and staff, conduct of staff with regard to drug company representatives and others who visit the practice, and many other issues that deal with the day-to-day operations and interactions of the people in the practice. Your HR person may be called upon to counsel staff members, to mediate disputes, to explain all of the legal and financial aspects of employment, to train employees or to work with a designated trainer, and to fire employees.

Human resources issues are complex and heavily regulated by local, state, and federal laws. Your HR person will need training and experience to perform this essential function for your practice.

## Finance Management

The financial aspect of your business as a medical practice is similar to other businesses. The organization exists, at least in part, to make money for those who work there. They should be paid for their services, and although there may not be a tremendous profit motive involved in the business, it should certainly afford the income that the people involved deserve based upon their training, experience, and abilities.

One difference between a medical practice and other business organizations is that most medical groups maintain their financial records on a cash basis rather than an accrual system. Most businesses now are established on an accrual system. *Cash basis* systems identify expenses when they are paid and income when it is received; *accrual* systems recognize expenses when they are incurred and income when it is earned.

Since most medical practices are privately owned organizations, they can still use the cash basis for their accounting systems. This is something that you should discuss with your accountant or CPA. There are accounting companies who specialize in accounting for medical practices.

Your accountant will provide invaluable assistance to you in setting up your payroll, accounts receivable, billing systems, and other financial control and audit functions. Your compliance with governmental and health care provider organizations is also vital to your accounting system. These are matters that can be dealt with by the experts in the accounting firms.

## *Information Technology Management*
The computerized medical practice is not only a thing of the present, but more and more the thing of the future as computer capabilities become ever more expansive. An *information technology* (IT) consultant will work with you, not only in setting up your practice and its computer needs, but also in helping you navigate the rapidly changing world of IT.

# chapter eleven:
# Fees, Billing, and Collections

Today, many new physicians join an established practice where fees, policies, standards, procedures, and treatments are in place. However, if you are starting your own practice, you need to figure out how much to charge and how to get paid.

## ESTABLISHING A FEE STRUCTURE

Your fee structure will be strongly influenced by local practices. The local medical association or your specialty practice association will be able to provide some guidance on establishing fees, and this is another place where good networking can be helpful. Other doctors and medical office managers will also have valuable information on fees.

You will need to establish fees for each of the services and procedures you offer to your patients—from complete physicals to tetanus shots, X-rays and other radiological services, blood draws, tests, surgeries, and so on. While many patients will be writing a check for their co-pay on the day of treatment, others may be required to pay larger sums. You may want to consider offering a day-of-service payment reduction for cash and checks, and a slightly smaller discount for credit card payments, since you will have to pay fees on credit card services. In either case, payment up front will save you billing time and money, and a small fee reduction can build goodwill among patients.

Depending on the size of your practice, your billing choices vary. Most doctors use a computerized billing system. This can be done with your own in-house billing department, or it can be done with an independent, computerized billing service bureau; both have several advantages. Whichever system you choose, it is absolutely critical that the entire billing process be in the hands of people who know what they are doing, have taken training on the subject, and can minimize the problems you face in dealing with the many different sets of procedures to collect your well-earned fees.

## IN-HOUSE BILLING

A money-wise decision will be to have a *billing manager* on your staff. The manager tracks the money coming in and going out of your office. The manager is there to document and track your claims, billings, and collections, and to handle personal interfacing with patients. Also, this person will not only ask questions about how to assist the patient in resolving any problems, but will also be an intermediary dealing with the patient's insurance company. This personal customer service benefits both you and your patients. More than one patient has left an office, not because of the doctor, but because of the poor handling of insurance claims and billing statements.

When the billing is internal, most corrections, delays, and problems that develop will be noticed much sooner, and then can be processed immediately by checking the patient's chart, consulting with the physician, or making a phone call to the patient or guardian. The claim or statement is corrected, mailed, re-billed, or faxed to the patient or insurance company without delay. Because your billing manager works only for your practice, he or she is more likely to take the time to make personal contacts with the patient and insurance companies, and to investigate until an error is corrected and the correct amount is paid.

Set standards regarding collection policies, and stick to them. All patient cases are different and require different investigation, but if you stick to your standards, it gives your staff security and groundwork to follow. It also takes much pressure and stress from the physician. Work closely with your billing manager.

# OUTSOURCE BILLING

An independent billing service will assign your account to a customer representative. This saves you office space, salaries, employee benefits, and other related expenses. In addition, if an account goes to collection, the agency serves as your intermediary between the patients, insurance companies, and collection agencies.

Most billing service customer representatives work on multiple accounts. The representative has a limited time frame to work on a doctor's accounts. If there are any errors to the account, it creates a delay of time and payment in order to get the correct information back and forth from office to office. Information can be delayed or lost. This can delay the financial response to the physician. It may also short-change the doctor due to the expense and charge for the services.

Most delays and errors are due to the human factor, such as the incorrect entry of Social Security numbers; incorrect or not updated insurance; and, wrong birth dates, addresses, or zip codes. Any one of these may delay the payment—sometimes for months.

Always check with your attorney before you sign a contract with a billing service or collection agency.

## *Superbill*

The *superbill* was designed to simplify clerical work for both the physician and the coder-entry person. It is to be placed into each patient's chart at the time of visit. This bill contains patient information, appointment information, Current Procedural Terminology (CPT) codes, diagnosis, and much more that all pertains to your visit and treatment of the patient, plus any payment information.

Superbill is effective only if you:
- always fill out a diagnosis;
- always check a procedure;
- always list symptoms, treatments, and medications;
- learn the difference between prolonged vs. consult service;
- do not use *rule out* for a diagnosis (i.e., rule out diabetes)— use symptoms;
- beware—well check-ups with sick diagnoses are rarely covered by insurance; and,
- charge add-on, same-day appointments as emergency visits.

The superbill is the recordkeeping procedure for each working day, and needs to be entered into the patient's computer records daily. From there, the Health Care Financing Administration (HCFA) claims or electronic claims go through your billing department, or the billing service company to the insurance company. Therefore, double-check your facts prior to turning in the superbill.

# OVERDUE PAYMENTS

At the end of every month, request a printed aging report from either the billing manager or your billing service representative. This keeps you updated on your practice as to where you are in accounts receivable. This aging report will give you information on each patient's outstanding insurance balance and how many months old his or her personal balance may be. This status information will allow you to:

- take effective control of deadbeats before they continue to run up more charges;
- make adjustments for patients whose finances are marginal before their balances are overwhelming; and,
- avoid the time, stress, and aggravation of trying to collect the overdue balance.

Here are several suggestions for improving collections.

- Give each patient your mission statement, policies, notice of privacy practice, and physician/patient arbitration agreement, along with other patient information sheets.
- When going over the forms with each new patient, the receptionist or nurse needs to state acceptable methods of co-payment and payment expectations at the time of each visit.
- Place a sign in an obvious area to remind established and new patients of the office policy, *payment due at time of visit.*
- Get superbills to the coder, and then to the HCFA or collection agency, as soon as possible to add to receivable accounts.
- Print out and send statements consistently on the same date each month. The statements should arrive no later than the fourth of each month. If you are in a large practice, then cycle statements out on the same week of each month. If statements are sent out in a random mailing, the patient usually pays randomly.

# DELINQUENT ACCOUNTS

In the standards you have set for your practice, decide the procedure for dealing with delinquent, overdue accounts. In almost any other business, a delinquent account may mean the loss of a house, car, or other item, but in medicine, due to insurance delays, payment is often many months in coming.

History shows that on the first statement, if the patient plans to pay, he or she does. The second statement is often a watershed. The third letter sets a firm date and states that after that date, all proper information will be sent to a collection agency and the patient is to deal with that company directly. Include the collection agency's phone number. After the date of expectancy, if there is still no payment, a call may be necessary. Be courteous and polite. Following is the suggested procedure for the conversation.

- Identify yourself and the name of the office from which you are calling. Be polite and courteous.
- Request to speak to the responsible party, and speak only to him or her.
- Greet the patient using his or her name.
- Ask if the letter was received and if the patient has any questions.
- Ask if payment has been sent and when.
- Ask if there is some problem that needs to be addressed.
- Does the patient plan to arrange payment? How much? How soon?
- State that if no payment is received by the date promised, this will go to collections.
- Avoid confrontations, arguments, and threats *no matter what.*
- Keep your word. Do not make demands unless you plan to follow through.

# Unpaid Bill Letter

[Letterhead]

_____
(address)

_____

_____

_____
(phone number)

Re: (Patient)_____

Dear (Patient)_____:

You have been sent in the recent past correspondence outlining the nature of the unpaid statements for our services.

You have given us no choice but to send the matter to (Collection Agency), and you should communicate with them in the future.

Under the circumstances, you can understand why we cannot continue your medical treatment.

Please let us know to whom you wish your charts to be sent.

Sincerely,


Dr. _____

# SKIPPERS

The *skip* patient is adept at running a balance with a doctor for all of his or her needs, then at statement time, skipping the payment by moving around and making it hard to find the paper trail. Some people are very good at this.

If you are using in-house billing, your office needs to first run down any leads via post office address changes, calls to work or cell numbers, and calls to any emergency numbers listed in the patient file. If this still comes to a dead end, make the necessary master copies of the patient's information as requested by your collection agency and fax them to the agency. They are now working for you in a detective capacity. Be sure to choose a reputable agency. Ask other doctors for references.

If your billing is handled by a billing service, your assigned representative at the billing service will be responsible for catching skips. They have a standard procedure to follow. The representative will make all the necessary copies and send them to you for approval. When it is approved, your office needs to send the papers back immediately to the billing service and they will turn them over to the collection agency. The agency will now become your detective. All this may take months. Be prepared for a lengthy wait for your share of the payment in either system.

# COLLECTION AGENCIES

You and your staff should strive to keep each patient's obligations to the practice at a minimum. The larger the account, the more difficult it is to pay off. If a patient, in spite of repeated reminders and requests, fails to pay on his or her account, one option is to send the account to a collection agency. Collection agencies make their money by taking a portion—usually a very substantial portion—of any amounts they are able to collect from your patients.

Sending matters out to a collection agency has its drawbacks. The collection agency has no interest in your patient/physician relationship, and sending an account for collection can be the end of that relationship. Collection agencies are concerned only about obtaining the money and their proportionate part of it. Although laws today require that they must be a little less direct in their tactics, collection agencies still apply pressure and can create an environment of hostility. That hostility can result in a patient or a former patient filing a complaint against you. Some problems that may occur in using a collection agency follow.

1. You may have no way of knowing if your office is becoming legally liable because the agency violated some federal or state statute, unless they choose to communicate it to you.
2. Even if the actions of the agency are legal, if they have been unethical or behaved in bad taste with any patients at any time it could come back to haunt you and your practice.
3. As long as your office stays legally and ethically consistent, the agency can do no less without overstepping those legal boundaries.
4. The agency account representative may be burdened with so many accounts that it will choose the smaller or easiest credit reports to work on and may delay the more difficult ones, although they are equally important to you.
5. Keep in mind, once the accounts have been turned over to the agency, it takes a negotiated percentage of all payments, be it insurance payments sent to the agency or payments from a patient who paid at the office.

Before you send an account for collection, talk with your accountant and your lawyer, especially if there is a large fee involved in the collection. Weigh your choices carefully and decide what is best for the practice.

# chapter twelve:
# Ethics

When a person is in the position to administer drugs and therapy, and perform surgery, that person is placed in a position of tremendous power and authority over the well-being of others. For this reason, it becomes absolutely necessary that stringent ethical standards be required.

Traditionally, the medical profession has established the highest ethical duties of the doctor toward the patient. That is why the doctor/patient relationship is held in such sacred status. A patient must be able to reveal everything to the physician in order to obtain the best medical advice. This is especially important in considering the issues of informed consent. The doctor cannot possibly give proper medical advice if the patient is not being completely candid with the physician, and may be unable to determine whether or not the patient's consent is an informed one. This medical advice may lead to life-changing decisions, and therefore, the patient should be expected to be completely forthright.

Although this is not a book devoted solely to ethics in the practice of medicine, it is important when beginning your medical practice that you learn some of the ethical considerations expected of you as the person in charge and responsible for the conduct of your practice. This responsibility extends to overseeing the conduct of the people working with you. It is your duty to maintain reasonable vigilance over those who work for you and maintain the high ethical standards expected in the medical profession. If you find technicians, nurses, nurse practitioners, physicians' assistants, colleagues, or staff cutting corners or doing things that are even slightly unethical, the best thing to do (for you and your practice) is to give them a warning. If they fail to heed the warning, tell them that they will be very happy working someplace else. If the conduct is egregious enough, they do not deserve a warning and should definitely be invited to find another place of employment.

You must not lose sight of the fact that the practice of medicine must also be run as a business. A doctor who has a reputation as an unethical practitioner will eventually have few, if any, patients, and will have to turn to some other endeavor to make a living.

It is difficult to be an ethical doctor. It is stressful, it is time-consuming, and it provides many temptations for dishonesty. However, the overwhelming majority of doctors succeed and thrive ethically.

## ETHICAL RULES

The American Medical Association provides the model rules for professional conduct, and the respective state jurisdictions also have rules of conduct. If someone's conduct, including yours, raises the slightest doubt as to whether or not it is ethical, then it is probably unethical.

If the question is close enough that you might want to have a discussion or seek an outside opinion, look to your medical association for guidance. Most associations have ethics hotlines or some other means of obtaining advice or counseling. The rules cannot be written to cover every unique situation. Instead, broad and general ethical rules must be interpreted and applied to the situation at hand.

A good suggestion for someone beginning a practice of medicine is to read the discipline reports contained in medical association publications and medical literature. It will take only a short time of examining these reports to learn how doctors can get into professional trouble or have their licenses revoked. They may be doing things that in other circumstances or professions would not be quite so important. For example, being arrogant, mean, or rude can generate a malpractice claim, particularly if it causes emotional distress in a patient. Also, if one doctor refuses to turn over a patient's charts to a new physician until the patient's bill is paid, it would be unethical. It is unethical for a doctor to deprive a patient of good medical care by withholding such medical records. The issue of the fee or bill is something quite different from the patient's health care and should be treated as such.

## ETHICS AND PERSONNEL

Another area where ethical considerations can be troublesome is in the invidious discrimination against individuals in employment, engagement for services, or other aspects of the practice of medicine. Such discrimination is defined by most jurisdictions as discrimination based upon race, gender, national origin, sexual orientation, religion, age, or disability. It is that discrimination that is so despicable that it offends the ordinary person's sensibilities. It is wise to keep all applications for employment and résumés of people who are interviewed for employment for at least two years in order to have your notes available explaining why someone was not hired.

The same standards can apply to your treatment of medical assistants, nurse practitioners, physicians' assistants, nurses, staff, and other doctors employed by you. Violations of these standards are governed by Title VII of the Civil Rights Act of 1964.

In selecting the people you interview for positions, remember that there are certain areas that you are ethically prevented from exploring, such as a person's age, marital status, ethnicity, or anything else that borders on such subject matter. Conversely, there are laws prohibiting you from hiring people who are in this country illegally, so it becomes a delicate balance as to how you gather necessary information without also violating someone's civil rights.

Making a decision as to whether or not a person should be hired can be challenging. You should focus on his or her training, technical experience, and previous employment. Contact all references, and listen carefully to what the references say about their former employee and why the person left employment there. These comments can be very helpful in determining whether or not a person will fit into your practice.

# UNAUTHORIZED PRACTICE OF MEDICINE

The people who work for you in your practice are there to support you in providing medical care for patients. Your decisions determine what kind of care the patients will receive. Medical assistants, nurses, physicians' assistants, nurse practitioners, and other staff may be of great help to you, but they are not to initiate medical care, only to follow your instructions in that regard.

They perform valuable tasks within the practice of medicine, but those tasks are done under your supervision. Your time is free for hospital visits, charting, attending medical meetings, and other things that they cannot do. Medical staff must practice within their scope of expertise and within proper guidelines. Most jurisdictions are very careful and concerned about doctors aiding and abetting anyone else in violation of professional rules of conduct, especially the practice of medicine without a license.

You should always remember that the doctors and staff who work under your supervision are your responsibility as far as ethics are concerned. This is particularly true if a doctor is under any form of medical disciplinary conditions that prevent the practice of medicine by that person. These doctors or former doctors are required to avoid the practice of medicine, but it is easy for them to slip back into practice. Be very careful in hiring and having these people work for you on medical matters. Avoid hiring former physicians or physicians under suspension to work in your practice as physicians' assistants, nurse practitioners, or in any way connected with the medical profession.

The unauthorized practice of medicine does not apply solely to other people; it also applies to you. You are trained and licensed to provide certain types of medical care to your patients. If you begin administering care in a field you are not qualified for, you are breaching medical ethics.

# DOCTOR RELATIONS WITH THE PUBLIC

It has been said that about 75% of physicians are introverts. This means that most physicians are not out glad-handing members of the public to drum up business or otherwise making themselves widely known in the community. Doctors usually are quite satisfied to maintain cordial relationships within their profession and build their practice through competent medical work, good personal relationships with patients, and word of mouth.

You have worked exceedingly hard to obtain your schooling, your medical education, and your training within some aspect of the field of medicine. People respect you because of your training, your accomplishments, and your position within the community.

Sometimes it is tempting to look with disdain on those who have not accomplished as much as you have. It is also tempting to become arrogant because you know more than most people do about very important things. Resist any temptation to show disdain, arrogance, or other antisocial attitudes. It is almost axiomatic that professional liability claims are made against physicians who have bad relationships with their patients.

In your relationships with the public as well as with your patients, you should remember that you are given a special privilege, even though you worked hard for it, of having knowledge, training, experience, and insight in the very important areas of keeping people healthy and alive. This is a humbling experience—not one to generate arrogance and insensitivity.

In many jurisdictions, doctors are protected from malpractice claims if they come to the rescue of people who are in some form of medical need. These *Good Samaritan laws* have a very important function. They represent the policy of that jurisdiction that people who are in extreme medical need can get help without exposing the helper to professional liability under extraordinary circumstances. Ethically, it is a physician's duty to help people in need, irrespective of such laws. The dilemma arises when you are in a jurisdiction that does not have such laws and you come across a person who is in need of medical care. If you turn your back and walk away, no one may know what you have done, except you. Therefore, it is your ethical decision whether or not to render such aid as may be necessary. It is suggested that you strongly consider rendering the aid required.

Doctors are subject to discipline if they are convicted of crimes or violations constituting acts of *moral turpitude*. Turpitude is defined as conduct that is base, vile, or depraved. Conduct that is unconnected with the practice of medicine, but is found to be of moral turpitude, can result in discipline. The state medical board must be notified of any actions against you as a doctor involving a felony or a misdemeanor. The American Medical Association, in its model rules, requires a doctor to report ethical violations of other doctors. You should seriously consider discussing such situations on an ethical hotline provided by your local medical association or state board. Reporting the conduct of other physicians and their staffs can be of great benefit to patients and the medical profession in your locality, but it must be done with discretion. Discussions with the proper personnel will be extremely helpful to you.

## SEX IN THE WORKPLACE

The relationship between doctor and patient is one of trust. If this trust is abused and the vulnerable patient is taken advantage of, the consequences may be disastrous for the doctor. Sexual relations with patients is prohibited. Regardless of the temptations, regardless of apparent mutual consent, regardless of whether it takes place in or outside your office, you must avoid having sexual relations with any of your patients at any time under any circumstances. In a case of *sexual harassment*, courts and juries do not make the fine distinction between harassment or discriminatory practices in the office or away from the office.

All jurisdictions have rules that strongly prohibit doctors from entering into sexual relationships with patients. Any sexual relationship may be construed as predatory in later testimony. This can occur in a disciplinary proceeding, a malpractice action, or in some other legal action.

This same prohibition must apply to having sexual relations with staff members. Although it may not be a violation of any of the ethical rules, it is extremely unprofessional and destructive conduct. Not only can such behavior set you up for a sexual harassment lawsuit, but it can undermine an efficient practice as coworkers become aware that a member of the staff is being treated differently and specially. Both you and the coworker lose the respect and esteem of other members of the staff. A charge of sexual harassment can ruin your reputation, your practice, your career, and your personal life.

Clearly, your staff must also abide by the same standards, avoiding liaisons with patients and with each other. They do not need to accept inappropriate behavior from patients. This is an area of highly subjective interpretations. A hand on the shoulder may be reassuring to one person and offensive to another. A hug or a shoulder rub, or even a pat on the bottom, may be given in the spirit of warmth and friendship, but predatory and inappropriate to the recipient. Err on the side of caution.

If you hire someone who creates a hostile work environment through the use of sexual harassment or discriminatory practices, document the incident, give a warning, and get rid of that person upon the next violation as soon as it occurs.

If a relationship between staff members, or between doctor and staff, should emerge based on true, honest, emotional feelings, the best solution for everyone concerned is to have the staff member leave employment and go to another place to work. This is a good example of how a practical solution for emotional and psychological dilemmas can also resolve potential ethical problems.

The paramount point for you to keep in mind is that you are the leader in your practice. All who work for you are looking to you for guidance. You set the standard. Ethical considerations are a daily concern, and you are expected to make ethical decisions constantly.

## DOCTOR/PATIENT FEE DISPUTES

You can expect disputes to arise between doctors and patients even when you have done everything possible to minimize them. Many jurisdictions have various ways of resolving such disputes, and among them are mandatory nonbinding arbitration, mediation, and mentoring. Be prepared to go through these procedures and do your best to extend the most professional courtesies to the patient, even though technically you may no longer handle his or her treatment needs.

When matters have reached that stage, the cost of collecting the money owed may far outweigh the original debt for fees. You might consider compromising on the fee. If it is not too large, you might consider abandoning it as quickly as you can, treating it as a bad debt. Confer with your tax advisor on the potential tax consequences of these decisions.

## CONFLICTS OF INTEREST

*Conflicts of interest* can be defined as situations in which a doctor has interests adverse to the patient's, and the exercise of those interests does some injury to the patient. Clearly, this situation arises when there is a fee dispute. The situation also arises if the doctor is in business with the patient. Conflicts of interest in that situation should be handled outside the medical practice because business relationships do not pertain to treatment by the doctor.

The doctor must exercise utmost loyalty to the patient, and that loyalty exists through the entire doctor/patient relationship. The duty of the doctor will end at the termination of the relationship, but the confidentiality of that relationship and the privileges attached to it do not end.

You should be very careful with respect to the sharing of information about the patient because of the HIPAA privacy requirements. A conflict of interest could arise if the information is requested and you are unsure as to what should be divulged. If the matter is serious enough, it seems the best conduct is to confer with legal counsel and get a written opinion regarding your course of action.

## TERMINATING A PATIENT

The relationship between doctor and patient is a very personal one, and as is the case in many other personal relationships, problems can arise. You have taken an oath to provide professional health care. If a patient is difficult and unruly, you cannot retaliate. A doctor must adhere to the standards of practice even though the patient's behavior is repugnant or despicable.

Terminating your relationship with a patient is a situation involving mixed emotions. If the matter has been handled successfully and the patient no longer needs your services, it is a happy departure and everyone leaves satisfied. If the contrary is true, the patient and you may both have difficulties in ending the relationship.

Whatever the reason for the termination, all files and charts belonging to the patient should be offered for transfer to another physician or to the patient, with a copy retained for your records.

If the patient demands the file or chart, holding it until fees are paid is a violation of professional ethics. Make a copy of the entire chart, give a copy of the chart to the patient, and make some other arrangement to obtain unpaid fees. Even the slightest suggestion of coercion by a doctor regarding a patient is ill advised.

After termination of a relationship, the question of how long you should maintain the patient's chart arises. You are responsible for a patient's chart that is destroyed prematurely, so it is wise to err on the side of caution. Some jurisdictions have limitations on how long a doctor should maintain a chart, but some do not. A good range is five to seven years. Electronic archiving now offers the option of storing files indefinitely.

The chart belongs to the patient, and after the applicable time or other limitations have expired, you should give your patient the opportunity to have the file sent to him or her. Patients will often say that they want you to keep it in your records. If that is the case, you must maintain it for them. The situation varies with the kind of treatment. For example, pediatric records should be kept until at least three to five years after the patient has reached 18 years of age.

If you purchase another doctor's practice, you may be responsible for maintaining that firm's files and charts. Whoever is left with the practice has that responsibility, and it could be somewhat burdensome. All of these issues are to be ironed out by negotiation and agreement before the problem gets out of hand.

If your practice closes its doors by merging with another practice or otherwise, what do you do with file storage when there is no successor firm to take over? There are storage companies that will maintain such files in safe environments, and the cost is relatively low. Nevertheless, you should make every effort to have your patients take the chart, and you should keep a copy for your records to protect yourself in case of malpractice in the future. If you cannot immediately locate your patient, you must make a reasonable effort to do so before you dispose of the file. You must show, through documentation, that you have exercised due diligence in your search.

You can imagine the dismay of a pediatrician or a family practice doctor being sued for malpractice sixteen to seventeen years after treating the patient, who was as a young child at the time. Having no chart or record of what was done could be disastrous. This points out the necessity for CD-ROM and other electronic storage as a backup, and you may even want to have more than just one backup for the records that go back that far.

Practicing medicine is not merely a matter of taking a patient and providing treatment. The doctor/patient relationship is one of a very personal nature. Trust and confidence are placed in the doctor by the patient, and the patient has the right to expect the doctor's best efforts to provide good care and effective medical procedures. In fact, the relationship between the doctor and the patient can become part of the treatment and the therapy for the patient.

# Patient Termination Letter

Date: _____

Address

Re: (Patient)_____

Dear (Patient)___:

Since (inception date)_____ we have enjoyed having a physician/patient relationship with you (your child). You are quite aware that an important part of medical care is cooperation of the patient in such care.

It appears that we no longer have the necessary cooperation from you, for whatever reason. We note that you:
- decline immunizations;
- fail to keep appointments;
- fail to keep your account current; and,
- have lost confidence in us.

For these reasons, we must decline to offer you any further medical treatment. We will notify your insurance, and will send your charts to whomever you request as soon as possible.

Thank you for the opportunity to serve you.

Sincerely,


Dr. _____

# chapter thirteen:
# Marketing Your Practice

Your practice of medicine will not thrive without patients. Do not make the mistake that some doctors have made by signing a lease for an office space; investing thousands of dollars in computers, furnishings, and medical equipment; hiring an office manager and a nurse; and then waiting for the patients to come through the door.

When you are beginning a practice, it is essential to have a business plan. Marketing your business is an important item in your business plan and your budget, and you should think of it as a vital part of your career building. While your marketing budget should not be calculated strictly as a percentage of gross revenues, established businesses typically spend 2%–5% of gross income on marketing, while new businesses may spend between 10%–15% of gross income for the first couple of years.

Marketing has two phases—getting patients and keeping them. In marketing your medical practice, you also have two audiences—the people or businesses that will be using your services directly, and the people or businesses that will be able to refer patients to you. For example, if you practice family medicine, your primary audience is the general public, but once you are established in the community, you may find that a lot of your business comes from insurance companies and other doctors. Your marketing should target both audiences.

In a small town, family connections and friends form the beginning network for your patient list. If you begin by buying an existing practice, you have a built-in basis not only for patients, but for a network upon which to build. When you purchase a practice, the patients may decide to stay with you or they may decide to switch to another doctor. Marketing can make the difference between the two decisions.

If you do purchase a practice or take over a practice in existence, consider having the outgoing or retiring doctor introduce you, through a letter, phone calls, or even an office open house where you can meet patients and they can meet you. If you are taking over a practice of a deceased doctor, take the time to compose a letter to the doctor's patients, expressing your condolences, introducing yourself, and inviting them to make an appointment to meet with you to discuss their future medical care.

Consider investing a modest amount of money in renovating the offices by putting in new carpeting and paintings, with some new furniture and decorations. An open house celebrating the change is a good opportunity to introduce yourself to the patients and to demonstrate to them that you are a person whom they can trust, just as the former physician trusted you.

Providing it meets the standards of your local medical association, you may also want to offer free initial consultations or screenings to potential clients. If you are new in the community, this opens the door and helps to build awareness of your service.

Your letterhead, business cards, brochure, website, prescription pads, and other materials that represent your practice's image are all a part of marketing. Getting professional design help on these materials can make a big difference in your public image. A designer can bring a level of sophistication to your practice that can convey a sense of competence and trustworthiness to your patients and potential patients.

Always ask your designer or printer for a final proof and read it over carefully. Read every single word and number. Your business card is useless if your name is misspelled or your phone number or email address is one number or character off. Do not assume that because the address is correct on your business cards, it is also correct on your letterhead and envelopes. Take time to proofread. If you do not and there is a typo, you will have to bear the cost and delays of reprinting your materials.

Your initial marketing materials should also include a formal announcement of the opening of your practice. This is typically a panel card, a single pane without folds, and matching envelopes. Use the best quality paper you can afford, ideally very similar to your business card. This is likely to be your first official piece of marketing for your practice, and it should reach the broadest possible audience—your contacts from medical school, other doctors, businesspeople in your community, family members, friends—in short, anyone who knows you or might be able to send patients your way.

## BUILDING A BASE

If you do not have an established base of patients, how do you build one? One of the basic methods of making contacts with potential patients is to join civic or charitable organizations and become active. This may include religious organizations, chambers of commerce, networking groups, charities, and even athletic clubs. Talk with people. Hand out business cards. Get interested in other people's lives. Before long, they will take an interest in yours.

## *Giving Lectures*

Acting as a speaker for civic organizations is a very good way of making yourself known as a doctor and an expert in your field. Take a page from presidential candidates, who drill themselves on every possible question that could be asked of them in a public forum. If you take the time in advance to imagine the worst-case scenario and the most devastating questions, and prepare yourself with answers, your public presentations will be a breeze.

Many hospitals have lecture programs for the community in which they invite specialists to address issues of common concern. When you affiliate with a local hospital, take the time to introduce yourself to the hospital's public relations staff and let them know you are available as a speaker or panelist.

You are competing with television and everything else that your audience could be doing instead of listening to you, so picking a good topic—and then delivering a great presentation—is your challenge. In deciding whether they will give up their lunch hour or their favorite detective show to come hear you talk, your potential audience will be asking themselves, "What's in it for me?" You have to provide information of value to your audience so they feel it was worth the sacrifice—and they will get the subtle message that you are someone who delivers on a promise.

It is up to you to make your presentation, whatever the subject matter, as thought provoking as possible. Prepare as thoroughly as you can. Rehearse your talk, add humor and visual aids (such as PowerPoint), and start and end on time. Consider putting together a handout that recaps the most important points of your presentation. Have your handout printed on your letterhead and attach a business card to it. Distribute it *after* your presentation. Carry plenty of additional business cards (you should be handing out at least ten a day as you are setting up your practice) and your brochure, if you happen to have one.

# ADVERTISING

For many years, doctors were prohibited from advertising their services, but today, you can find ads for medical services on television, in print, on the radio, on the Internet, and even on billboards. Before you invest in any advertising, check the AMA code of ethics and your state medical board business and professions code.

In general, your ads must contain no inducements, no guarantees, and offer no discounts or payments to attract patients. The AMA Code of Ethics section E-5.02 states:

*There are no restrictions on advertising by physicians except those that can be specifically justified to protect the public from deceptive practices. A physician may publicize him- or herself as a physician through any commercial publicity or other form of public communication (including any newspaper, magazine, telephone directory, radio, television, direct mail, or other advertising) provided that the communication shall not be misleading because of the omission of necessary material information, shall not contain any false or misleading statement, or shall not otherwise operate to deceive.*

Whether your marketing works or not depends largely on whether your materials are carefully targeted to your audience of potential patients, whether the materials say something of interest to that audience, whether they are well crafted and have aesthetic appeal, and how regularly the potential patient hears from you or sees your name. Your marketing can take a variety of forms, and for best effect, should probably take several different approaches. Among your options are:

- Yellow Pages advertising;
- local newspaper and magazine advertising;
- ' website;
- brochure;
- direct mail;
- radio or television advertising; and,
- press releases.

Your goal in each of your marketing efforts is to remind the community that you are there and to inspire them to call you. One of the best ways to do this is to provide useful information. Whether that takes the form of tips for avoiding tick bites or reminders to get a colonoscopy, these messages express your interest in the community's well-being. They can be incorporated into almost any form of promotion that you do, whether it is your practice website, your regular column in the local newspaper, personal letters to current, past, and potential patients, or the other marketing methods listed above.

If you have a well-defined area of expertise and reasonable writing skills, you may consider writing articles for consumer publications. For example, if you are an expert in pediatric cardiology, you could write an article entitled, "The Ten Most Important Warning Signs of Childhood Heart Problems." You would probably not be paid for the article, but it would reach your target audience, and your name and contact information would appear as part of your credit.

Depending upon your practice, you may wish to produce a brochure, though a website may be a better investment for a young practice. Quality brochures are costly to produce and difficult to update. In general, a brochure, whether paper or electronic, should outline your practice's philosophy, areas of specialty, and credentials. Unlike ads, which reach out to your audience, brochures and websites are more passive marketing. They are complementary to all of the other marketing you do and should not be relied upon as your sole means of promotion. Work with a professional designer to create an image that will appeal to your patients. Keep text simple, direct, short, and easy to read. Of course, proofread, proofread, proofread.

A website can be a tremendous asset to your practice. It can provide in-depth information on you, your practice, and your specialty, as well as illustrations and reference material that can help your patients make informed decisions. If you find that your office staff is answering the same questions over and over on the phone, you can post the answers to those questions on your website. You can include links to articles that you have written and hospitals with which you are affiliated. Your website also gives you a platform for expressing your opinion on controversial treatments, and for offering health care tips and seasonal reminders.

Press releases are succinct who-how-when-what-where alerts to the local media that something of interest is going on in your practice. Some small community newspapers will use press releases verbatim; other papers, if the subject is newsworthy, will assign a reporter to contact you, find out more, and write an article. The beauty of press releases is that they are free. Simply call the publication, ask for the name of the person who handles health (or another subject, depending on your specialty), write the press release, and mail or email it to that person. If you send a photograph, your press release is more likely to get picked up by the media. Make sure that the subject is newsworthy. Depending on the size of your community, opening a new office, giving a lecture, offering free blood pressure testing, offering flu shots, offering free water safety cards, or many other things you do could be considered newsworthy. An article in the local paper can build your credibility, increase your name awareness, and attract patients.

## KEEPING PATIENTS

Once you have patients and referral sources, you need to keep them. All of the marketing in the world will not make up for bad service, so your first concern should be to deliver the best professional service you possibly can.

Returning phone calls is a critical component of your marketing program. If you fail to return phone calls, answer letters, or reply to emails, you are undermining everything else you do to promote your business.

Get in the habit of saying thank you. When you get a referral, whether it comes from another doctor, a family member, a friend, or someone else, take the time immediately to express your appreciation. A handwritten thank-you note is the most gracious way to do this, but a phone call or email, or even a well-written form letter, will suffice. Do not wait to see if the referral turns into a patient. Express your appreciation for the thought.

Networking with colleagues also helps to keep your business alive. Plan to have lunch at least once a week with a colleague you do not see very often. These lunches do not need to be formal or have an agenda. They merely keep the lines of communication open and keep you fresh in the minds of your important contacts. For example, pediatricians should keep in contact with obstetricians and gynecologists, and cardiologists should do the same with internists and family medicine specialists.

Marketing is a process, not an event. It is cumulative, each successive contact building on the reader/viewer/listener's last contact with your name or message. Be consistent and regular in your marketing. It is better to spend small amounts over a long period of time than to waste your annual budget on one television or print ad. You are building an image, helping potential patients to feel that they know you and can trust you. Just like your face-to-face contacts with patients, that process takes time, but can yield positive results for years to come.

Whatever forms of marketing you are considering, remember— you are a doctor, not a marketing executive. Talk to a marketing professional—other doctors or your local medical association may be able to make a referral—and decide which marketing methods will be most effective for you, given your practice goals and your budget.

Marketing is as important to the life of your practice as is medical competence. Regardless of how brilliant or experienced you are, if you have no patients, you have no practice.

chapter fourteen:

# Medical-Legal Issues

The concerns of societies regarding physicians and their patients have been dealt with since the earliest civilization, that of the Sumerians. These concerns were expressed in their laws, which were carried over into the well-known Code of Hammurabi, named after the Babylonian conqueror of the Sumerians. Later, in Egyptian papyri, rules were set out prescribing severe punishment for physicians who treated their patients improperly.

Additionally, severe admonitions are found in the writings of Aesculapius, Hippocrates, and in the Judeo-Christian heritage of ethics. These considerations are found throughout English common law, which forms the foundation of the legal system in the United States.

Issues surrounding the relationship between physician and patient are some of the most complex you will face. They often go far beyond your expertise and experience as a doctor into serious areas of the law. Your awareness of and adherence to the laws that regulate these complex issues is an essential element in the foundation and successful growth of your practice. Legal-medical aspects of medical practice are addressed below in the following categories: the physician/patient relationship, physician/patient communications and privileges, patients' rights of privacy, HIPAA, informed consent, the physician as witness, and professional liability.

# THE PHYSICIAN/PATIENT RELATIONSHIP

When a physician accepts a request to provide medical services, the physician/patient relationship begins. Such a request from a patient or guardian may be either implied or expressed. Generally, it is held that the relationship begins when an assistant or other person working for the physician makes an appointment in response to the patient's request.

There are, however, exceptions to this general rule. For example, the rendering of first aid in an emergency does not usually establish a physician/patient relationship, particularly in states with Good Samaritan laws. One visit for a purpose that is accomplished at that visit does not establish such a relationship either, provided that there is mutual agreement that the relationship has not been established. This is also true for a single emergency room visit that requires no follow-up treatment or if the patient is specifically referred to another source for the follow-up treatment.

When the physician/patient relationship is established, the physician must provide continuing care to the patient as long as the patient's condition necessitates such care, and must keep the patient informed of the nature of the condition and all aspects of treatment. The patient is expected to participate responsibly in such care as well.

The termination of the physician/patient relationship can occur in several ways. Commonly it is when the condition reaches a clinical end point and the physician's services are no longer needed. The physician should make it clear that there is no need for the patient to return, and the patient must understand and accept this decision.

The relationship may also terminate unilaterally at the request of either party. The physician always bears a certain responsibility because of special knowledge of the medical circumstances and must be alert for ambiguous situations, such as the patient who follows some advice but not all, or one who misses one appointment and then keeps the next, and continues in this pattern.

There is no excuse for a doctor's failure to keep a patient informed of the current status of the matter that the doctor is handling. If the patient fails to keep appointments or otherwise disappears from the practice, it is the doctor's duty to make a reasonable effort to contact the patient. This is so even if the condition for which the patient is being treated is not life threatening. Reasonable efforts should be made to contact the patient if an appointment was necessary but was not kept. These efforts should include some form of communication of record, such as a letter or an email that will indicate that you are trying to contact the patient and expect a response. Your documented efforts will come in handy if there is trouble later on.

When a patient is sent for consultation and continuing care, and it is not clear to the patient or the consultant whether the referring physician has ceased to assume responsibility, another ambiguity arises. It is the duty of the physician to clarify any ambiguities that the patient or the situation suggests. When the relationship is terminated, the physician must make an effort to ensure that the patient is receiving competent care on a continuing basis from another source and that the pertinent records are made available to the new physician.

Letters of termination should be very specific in setting out the reasons for the termination, and should be phrased to avoid creating any antagonism or animosity. You may obtain sample letters of termination from the General Counsel's Office of the American Medical Association (AMA). These forms provide guidelines that you can modify to suit the circumstances of your cases. Make certain that the original is sent certified mail, return receipt requested, because you want to have a record that the patient received the letter. The signed receipt is attached to the copy of the letter, which is inserted in the patient's chart.

## PHYSICIAN/PATIENT COMMUNICATIONS AND PRIVILEGES

The relationship between physician and patient creates a special privilege in the law. This privilege is based upon the policy of the law that the physician must possess as much information as possible in order for the proper care and treatment to be given. The patient must feel free to reveal all information and be confident that it will not be revealed to anyone except the caregivers working with the physician. The privilege belongs to the patient. It may be revoked only by the patient except for certain circumstances. One of these exceptions is when information must be released according to law, as in cases of certain communicable diseases, stab or gunshot wounds, and suspected child abuse.

In some jurisdictions this may extend to situations in which the patient threatens the health of another person or appears to be suicidal. Another exception is disclosing the limited information requested by medical providers. This has been held to be authorized by the implied consent of the patient who requests the third party to compensate the physician for the medical services rendered. Another exception is the situation where the patient reveals information to a third party not assisting in the medical care. In that case, revocation of the privilege is implied.

The privilege of the physician/patient relationship is waived in most jurisdictions automatically when a lawsuit is filed claiming personal injury. This waiver enables the defendants to examine the medical history of the patient and the general background of the patient who is seeking compensation for medical treatment for injuries. Notwithstanding this release, a signed authorization should be presented, or a subpoena served with respect to such records and charts.

Problems regarding physician/patient privilege can take a number of vexing forms and present the doctor with dilemmas. Your local medical association may be able to assist you in resolving these issues or you may wish to go directly to counsel. Following are a number of situations where matters of privilege are not clear cut.

In one case, the physician may be told that the information must be released because a lawsuit has been filed, but the information is privileged. For example, if the plaintiff is seeking damages for emotional distress, the records of psychologists and psychiatrists may be relevant. If no such damages are sought, such medical records may not be relevant and may not be revealed.

Second, it is not just the information given by the patient that is privileged, but all information learned from any source about the patient. For example, the physician may have conversations with other health care providers, such as psychologists, psychiatrists, or even law enforcement agencies.

A third dilemma is that the information may not be disclosed to the patient's spouse or other close relatives unless the patient is unable to comprehend the surrounding circumstances. For example, if the medical records indicate that a spouse was given medical treatment for a venereal disease, a physician should seek advice of counsel before revealing such information.

A fourth dilemma is that the privileged status of the information continues after the patient's death. In all cases, you should obtain a signed release specifically referring to the information in question, and if you have any doubts, seek legal counsel's advice.

# THE PATIENT'S PRIVACY RIGHTS

Patients have the same constitutional rights of privacy as anyone else. Even though a patient submits to an examination or other medical procedures, he or she still has the right not to have anyone except those necessary to the procedure present and not to have a picture taken. Written consent to have observers present, even medical students and residents who are not directly concerned with the care, or have pictures taken (video, film, or still photographs), must be obtained. Often, a broad consent to these procedures and photographs is obtained upon admission to the hospital.

It is important for the patient to be told about what is being waived to ensure that you do not face an angry patient later on and perhaps even a lawsuit. Most patients are very understanding, and even enthusiastic about being a part of the instruction of medical students by way of rounds, film, or photographs. There are standard forms available from the General Counsel's Office of the AMA that you may obtain and use so that you are protected.

# HIPAA

*The Health Insurance Portability and Accountability Act of 1996* (HIPAA) gave authority to the Department of Health and Human Services to adopt new rules protecting patients' privacy. The Department published the regulations, and compliance took effect on April 14, 2003.

From that date forward, physicians have been required to adopt policies for obtaining patients' permission to disclose confidential information. The HIPAA privacy regulations preempt existing state laws covering confidential medical records unless such state laws are more stringent.

The federal HIPAA rules create patients' rights, which include:
- the right to consent for the use of or disclosure of demographic information, such as name, address, Social Security number, and other identifying information, as well as confidential information;
- the right to be given a description of all the intended uses and disclosures of patient information, with examples, before signing the consent form. This privacy practices notice is specified in the regulations, and must be written in plain language to be easily understood by patients and families. This also requires translations or interpretation in most states;
- the right to authorize or withhold authority for uses and disclosures other than for normal purposes, such as treatment, payment, or operations. An example would be use of such information for fundraising by the hospital;
- the right to receive an accounting of all disclosures and a specification as to when, what, to whom, and why disclosures were made;

- the right to require restrictions on the use and disclosure of patient information; and,
- the right to have these requirements apply to both written and oral communications, as well as electronically stored and transmitted confidential patient information.

The rules and requirements of HIPAA may be modified from time to time. The HIPAA forms and current rules and regulations can be obtained from your local medical association or the American Medical Association, which can also give guidance on their use. You can also get assistance on HIPAA issues from your professional liability insurer.

# INFORMED CONSENT

Under English common law, which forms the basis of most American law, a harmful or offensive touching constituted an element of a tort or civil action called battery. A defense to the tort was consent to such touching. Many medical services could not be performed without touching. In order for the patient to give consent for such touching, the physician must inform the patient of the need for and potential results of such touching. Then the patient may give consent truly because the patient has been informed of the potential consequences of such touching.

The patient must be sufficiently mentally competent to understand the explanation of such consequences. The nature of the illness being treated, the procedure or treatment itself, its probable benefits and major risks, as well as the alternative means of treatment with their benefits and risks, must be explained clearly so that the patient can make an informed choice.

If the patient is unconscious, under the influence of drugs or medication, or emotionally disturbed, the method of obtaining consent should be that set forth in the law of your jurisdiction, which will also guide you if the patient has not reached majority.

The exceptions to obtaining informed consent are few, and these are also specified in individual state laws. One that is common to all states is an emergency situation threatening the patient's life when obtaining an informed consent would be inappropriate or impossible.

Keep in mind that all of these situations are subject to scrutiny and examination after the fact. In deciding what information to include in the explanation, the physician is guided by the principle of what is best for the patient.

Remote or improbable risks or consequences of a treatment or procedure are not necessary to be given. Those that are reasonable to disclose in view of the patient's emotional and physical condition are all that is required. If either a mental or physical condition seriously limits the information that can be given to the patient, a reasonable disclosure should be given to the patient's spouse, or to the nearest relative if there is no spouse.

Such consent must be worded specifically for each situation and obtained for a wide variety of treatments and procedures. Some of these may be surprising, such as the disposition of removed organs or amputated limbs, the spouse's consent for abortion and sterilization, use of drugs under clinical investigation, blood transfusions, and treadmill stress tests, as well as procedures that could qualify as experimental.

At no time should a doctor give an implied or express guarantee of results during such an explanation or on the consent form. When treatment involves complicated and serious procedures, the use of a tape-recorded explanation or a videotaped session explaining these procedures may be beneficial. In such a situation, you must be careful to have your information in written form to be certain that you cover all of the details. Make sure that the written materials are attached to the chart along with the videotape or audiotape.

Always obtain informed consent, and assume that it will always be required when you must deal with touching the patient in any way, even taking blood pressure. Just as important is the patient's knowledge of the HIPAA requirements, and you must make sure that both of these things are noted in the patient's chart. The discussions with regard to consent may be on an audio- or videotape, and may be with a guardian or conservator. This is particularly true when treating minors.

Patients whose primary language is not English present a challenge if you do not speak their language. Sometimes such people are very proud of their limited ability to speak English. They will tell you that they understand your explanations when they really do not. You are going to have to be especially diplomatic and adept at determining the patient's degree of understanding and whether or not an interpreter is required in order to secure informed consent.

## ADVANCE DIRECTIVES

One important practice area that seems to get more attention in the media than in medical education is the matter of *advance directives*. Every day, doctors are confronted with confounding and painful decisions about their patients because the patients have no written documents outlining their preferences for care. The media attention is good, because it gets more people thinking about the value of advance directives, but thinking about it is not the same as doing it, and many patients will need to be encouraged to actually take the step of putting their wishes onto paper.

As you are setting up your practice, you have an opportunity to put systems in place that make this subject a normal and increasingly easy and open matter for discussion with your patients. You can educate your patients about the value of advance directives—or at least initiate the conversation. That may mean adding a couple of questions to your intake form: *Do you have a written advance directive for health care? Do you have a written durable power of attorney for health care?* It may also mean opening a conversation by asking the question, *Have you thought about how you would like your doctor and your family to handle your care if you should become temporarily or permanently unable to care for yourself?*

Advance directives should become part of the patient's file. You should devise some indicator on the front of the file to alert anyone who opens it that this patient has an advance directive. Advance directives can be easily scanned into a patient's electronic health record to become a permanent part of the file, following the patient wherever he or she goes. It is up to physicians to guide their patients into making—and putting into writing—such critical decisions about their care.

# THE PHYSICIAN AS WITNESS

As a physician, you may become a witness under at least three sets of circumstances: (1) you participated in providing medical care for a patient and must testify as to the facts in that treatment, either in a criminal trial or in a civil trial; (2) you are an expert witness, having never treated the patient; and, (3) you are a defendant in a malpractice lawsuit.

Your testimony in a criminal trial may be forensic, calling upon your expertise in determining, for example, the cause or time of death or the circumstances surrounding the injuries that people have suffered. This may also involve testimony with regard to molestation of children. The testimony you may give in a civil case may have to do with personal injury and wrongful death and an opinion as to the connection of an injury or death from the acts of others. The most important thing to remember is to keep accurate medical records and to be sure that others involved in the patient's care do so as well.

A physician learns about being a witness by the receipt of a subpoena for the production of medical records. This is often accompanied by a requirement to appear for a deposition or hearing.

A subpoena serves notice to a proposed witness that the court is exercising its jurisdiction to require that a penalty for failure to comply may result. The power exercised by the court in the issuance of the subpoena is pervasive and will be enforced without exception. There may be some extenuating circumstances where the relief of the subpoena may be obtained or modified, such as terminal illness, physical incapacity, and mental or emotional disturbance.

Attempting to avoid a subpoena is futile. Accept the subpoena and then, if necessary, seek some arrangement as to the time and place of the appearance to accommodate your schedule. It may also be possible to videotape your deposition. Whenever you are subpoenaed as a witness, consult your lawyer, be certain that your records are accurate and complete, and under no circumstances alter them whatsoever. Ask your lawyer if a release is required from the patient. The written authorization of the patient is almost always necessary. Have the details of your credentials in mind, including dates, such as graduation from medical school, admittance to practice in a certain jurisdiction, and things of that kind.

If your testimony is required as an expert witness, you will have ample advance notice of your involvement and will have discussed the case thoroughly with counsel for the side that called you as a witness. Most jurisdictions provide that an expert witness be given a fee in advance. These arrangements are made between the physician and the attorney who is seeking the testimony. Expert fees vary quite widely, so you should ask the local medical association or bar association what the prevailing fee is in your area for your specialty. You can be called as an expert witness regardless of your level of experience as a physician.

Expert opinion evidence is weighed by the jury, which means that they may assign relatively little or great importance to it. They do not regard it in the same light as they do objective, direct, or circumstantial evidence, but many times expert opinion is the only way certain evidence can be given to the jury. Moreover, it may be the only way the jury can understand the basic issues in a case, particularly when personal injury or medical malpractice is involved.

*Expert testimony* is an exception to the evidence rules disallowing opinions, and makes it possible for those who have education, experience, and other exposure to a certain subject beyond that of the average person to give an opinion on a narrow subject matter.

An expert witness in a malpractice case must testify as to the standard of care in the community for that particular kind of medical procedure under the same or similar circumstances. It must be established that you know the standard of care and have a foundational knowledge enabling you to express an opinion on the standard of care. Then, you must testify with respect to the facts in the case and how those facts comply or do not comply with that standard. By casting the facts in relief against the standard of care, you will be expected to express an opinion as to whether or not the conduct of the physician or other health care practitioner is within or below that standard of care.

In all circumstances, when you are testifying, follow these guidelines.

- Always tell the truth. State all that is pertinent in a succinct and accurate way, without embellishment.
- If you do not know the answer, admit that you do not.
- Be sure you understand the question before answering it. If you do not understand it, say so immediately. A lawyer questioning you will rephrase it or ask the court reporter to read it back.
- Take the time you need to think about the question and to formulate your answer before responding. Do not be rushed.
- Answer the question that is asked and then stop. Do not volunteer information that is not directly related to the answer.
- Look at your lawyer only when your lawyer is asking a question or talking to you or to the court. You are on your own and you will not get any help from the lawyer or the judge when you are answering questions put to you by the other side.
- Speak so that everyone can hear you, and keep your hands away from your mouth. Always give an audible answer so the court reporter can record it. Do not nod your head affirmatively or negatively, or use your hands to indicate direction or size.
- If you must make an estimate, make certain that everyone understands that you are estimating.
- Always be courteous. Answer "yes, sir," and "no, ma'am," and address the judge only as "Your Honor."

- Do not argue with the lawyer on the other side. The lawyer has a right to question you within the limits of propriety set by the court. Try to remain calm and do not lose your temper, no matter how you are provoked.
- If you are asked whether or not you have talked to the lawyer who engaged you or to an investigator, admit it freely if it is the truth.
- Your attempts at humor are very dangerous. A lawsuit is a serious matter and all concerned are serious, particularly the jury. Since the jury has the choice of believing or not believing percipient witnesses, but must weigh the value of expert opinion witnesses, you want to maintain your credibility as an expert witness. If you treat your role frivolously, your credibility with the jury plummets and they will give your testimony very little weight.
- Make only very brief eye contact with members of the jury while you are testifying.
- Your demeanor should reflect a search for the truth. The courtroom is not a theater, or a place to manifest your ego, or a place to demean an attorney who apparently does not know as much about medicine as you do. Lawyers quite often know just enough to try the case.
- Do not let the lawyer on the other side catch you by asking you whether you are willing to swear to what you have said. You were sworn to tell the truth and it is assumed that your answers to questions are testimony under oath.

# PROFESSIONAL LIABILITY

The considerations involved in professional liability are as important to a medical practice as marketing and other commercial aspects of the practice. A medical practice can be destroyed by excessive professional liability assaults brought about by claims and lawsuits.

Therefore, these materials are set out here as extremely important aspects of the success of your professional practice, as well as your success as a business. It has been said conflict resolution skills are as important to a doctor's success as training to be a good clinician, but no one has put resources into that at a national level. That emphasis is put here in a business context because that is where it belongs.

The population shift from rural areas to cities has weakened the personal relationship between physicians and their patients that often existed in smaller communities. Patients now depersonalize the physician somewhat and the physician may do the same to the patients.

Litigation has become a more acceptable means of resolving disputes because of the depersonalization of physicians. This increase has resulted in more of a demand for lawyers who specialize in medical-legal matters. There is a large number of such lawyers who are very sophisticated in medical matters and who are eager to pursue litigation in this area. As a result of rapid advances in communications, standards of practice are no longer limited to the local community. Such standards of practice or care can now be national or even international.

The increasing sophistication of the field of medicine means that physicians are undertaking treatment or procedures that carry high risk. It also means using treatments that are not in themselves risky on patients who are in much more serious condition, and consequently, at higher risk. In both sets of circumstances, risk is increased.

There are few people who contend that physicians are contributing to a crisis in medical, professional liability through decreasing competence. In fact, the indications are that doctors are becoming more competent. Nevertheless, physicians must do more to keep their own houses in order and eliminate incompetence wherever it is encountered. One of the important ways that the profession maintains and increases the level of competence is through *mandatory continuing medical education.* These courses or seminars are required in most jurisdictions, and are very useful to every physician. They should be looked upon as a benefit rather than as drudgery.

Whatever the causes of professional liability, the result for physicians is higher malpractice premiums and a diminishing number of insurance carriers willing to write professional liability policies. Premiums have risen enormously over the past few years. In some parts of the country, the annual premiums are going up even higher for specialties such as neurosurgery, obstetrics, and orthopedics.

Before getting into what you should do if you are sued and how to reduce the likelihood of a suit, a few other points need to be mentioned. Review your insurance coverage with your insurance broker to make sure it is the best available for you. Your broker is a professional with education and experience far different from yours, but very valuable to you.

In some jurisdictions, if there is a conflict between the insurer and the insured, the insurer must pay reasonable fees for the insured's choice of an attorney. Discuss your exposure with your attorney. Look over your assets together. Consider items that could be in trust or otherwise protected. Keep in mind that if you are transferring property to protect it from a pending or threatened lawsuit, such transfers may be set aside or vacated as conveyances under fraudulent circumstances. It is crucial for you to protect your assets as much as possible with proper legal advice long before you have even the hint of a professional liability question.

What do you do when you are sued? The first thing to do is notify your insurance company by telephone and follow up immediately in writing. (Sometimes this is done through your broker.) Quickly call your attorney. If you are served with a summons and complaint, do not try to avoid it. Service may be made by publication when it is determined that a defendant is clearly attempting to avoid service. In other words, service may be accomplished at a time when you are not aware, and therefore, you lose your control over when the time starts to run. If you are actually served, your attorney can ask for extensions of time and other accommodations. Your attorney may be in a position to give accommodations to the other side later on as well, and will want to start a relationship that is professional.

Review the patient's records. Make sure they are complete, including all lab and X-ray reports. Under no circumstances should you make any changes or alterations in the records, even if it seems that you can clarify notes or include something that you "thought" or "knew" but forgot to include. Doing so may make the whole case go sour for you, even if you did nothing wrong. Make no oral or written statements to anyone about the case without talking to the attorney who is appointed for you by your insurance carrier and your own attorney. Make a copy of your records and keep the copy in your safe-deposit box. Keep the original in your office under lock and key.

When a plaintiff files a complaint and serves it, the defendant must then file a written pleading. This is usually filed by your attorney on your behalf along with the attorney that is hired by the insurance company. By contract, the insurance company can supervise the litigation, determine what should take place during the litigation, and may retain power to settle the case, but only with your consent. When obtaining your medical malpractice insurance, make certain that your broker shows you the specific provision in the policy that provides for your consent before the company can settle the case.

Once you become a defendant, you may expect the plaintiff to take your deposition. The deposition is held outside of the court for the purpose of discovering facts about the case and preserving testimony. *Deposition* testimony is as important as courtroom testimony, and should be treated with the same seriousness and gravity as courtroom testimony. It is testimony under oath of you as either witness or party to a lawsuit and it is like testimony in the court itself. In most jurisdictions, the deposition may be used for any purpose in litigation, and you must remember at all times during your deposition that what you are saying is being written down and can be read to the court or the jury.

You have the right to have your deposition taken to suit your schedule, both personal and professional, and this is usually accomplished by the attorneys on both sides. If they cannot arrange for this for you, the court will do so in most instances.

Additionally, you have the right to see all the medical records involved in the case ahead of time to prepare for your deposition. You should review the case thoroughly in conference with your lawyer and the lawyer assigned to you by the insurance company before you appear for the deposition. It may only be necessary for you to discuss the case with the lawyer hired for you by your insurer. Under no circumstances whatsoever should you allow yourself to be deposed without your lawyer present. Your testimony may come back to haunt you in court.

All the parties have the right to be present at all depositions. Attorneys for both sides are always there, and so is a court reporter. The opposing party is entitled to copies of all documents that a witness uses to refresh recollections. If you plan to use any, show them to your lawyers and discuss them ahead of time. You will have an opportunity at a later date to review the deposition transcript after it has been typed and to make any corrections you wish. Remember that any substantial changes can erode your credibility as a witness if the transcript is read to the jury with and without the changes.

The most trying situation for you as a physician may be when you are testifying as a defendant in your own professional liability case. Your intelligence, education, judgment, and skill—most of what you rely upon as a physician—are being called into question. The other side may even have a well-qualified physician who will testify under oath that you are below the standard of care in your handling of a particular patient.

Even so, it is helpful to your case if you can be present during the entire trial, from the selection of the jury through opening statements, the presentation of evidence, the arguments of counsel, and to the instruction of the jury. It not only helps you in preparing for your own testimony, but your presence may help your case in the minds of the jury, because they will become aware that you are treating it seriously. That is a signal that they should do so as well. It demonstrates your humanity and helps the jurors think of you more personally, rather than just as some person who showed up now and then and looked disinterested. Always remain a calm observer. Expressions of anger or disbelief will interfere with the process and will hurt your case. The key words are equanimity and objectivity—you must seem to be keenly interested but not overly emotionally involved.

If you are involved in a professional liability claim, you must make an intelligent determination as to whether you should consent to settlement. There will be enormous pressure to settle placed upon you by your insurer, your counsel, and the court. Only you can decide whether you are going to consent to a settlement.

You must keep in mind that medical malpractice settlements must be reported, not just to state or local authorities, but to the national medical malpractice index. These reporting requirements are helpful to the public and were enacted by the government after a great deal of pressure from the public.

As a consequence, you must weigh the pressure to consent to settlement very carefully. Keep in mind that an expert in your field has formed an opinion that you acted below the standard of care. This could result in a judgment against you for professional liability, and such a judgment will become a matter of public record. Only limited information regarding a settlement will become public record.

On the other hand, people can order transcripts of testimony from your trial and look at the documents that are on file. These files are open to the public. It is sometimes horrifying to physicians to learn that when they are sued for the second time, counsel for the plaintiff has a complete transcript of the physician's first trial deposition and court testimony with which to prepare for the second lawsuit. All of these things must be factored into your thinking when you decide whether to consent to settle or not.

Above all, you want to consider first the welfare of the patient. This is true even though you may think the patient is a greedy ingrate who wants to take advantage of a lawsuit to avoid paying you or is angry at life and has suddenly found a way to blame someone for all of life's troubles. It is a complicated matter, and you must think of yourself and your family as well.

There have been attempts by many states to change their laws in the area of tort reform. One of the changes suggested is that the statute of limitations begins to run from the date of injury, not of discovery. Another is to require summary judgments in cases where there is no material disagreement on the facts. In this way, a judge could decide a case without a lengthy hearing and expensive attorney's fees on both sides.

Remember that the judge decides legal issues and the jury decides factual issues. If both sides agree on the factual issues, there is no need for a jury, and the court can decide the legal issues alone. There are occasions where a court may want to have a jury to advise the court in deciding factual issues, but this is discretionary with the court. Most courts do not want to involve a jury if they can avoid it. The expense of jury trials is something that everyone wants to avoid—including the courts. In some jurisdictions, joint and several liability has been done away with so that a physician would be held liable only for the portion of damages attributed to that physician. This is not true in all jurisdictions, and is another reason why you should discuss these things with your legal counsel.

Approximately 75% of all medical malpractice cases that go to trial result in a verdict in favor of the doctor.

# ANATOMY *of a*
# PROFESSIONAL LIABILITY TRIAL
*Time Line of Events from Pre-filing of Complaint to End of Appeal and Satisfaction of Judgment*

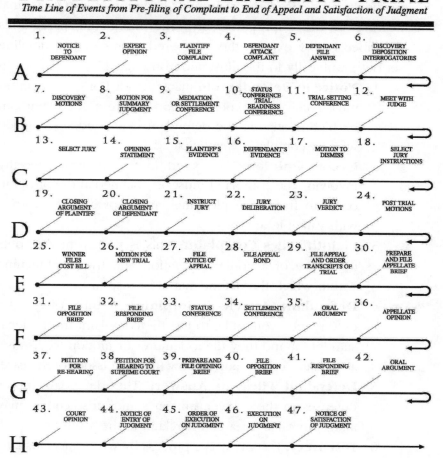

**A**
1. NOTICE TO DEFENDANT
2. EXPERT OPINION
3. PLAINTIFF FILE COMPLAINT
4. DEFENDANT ATTACK COMPLAINT
5. DEFENDANT FILE ANSWER
6. DISCOVERY DEPOSITION INTERROGATORIES

**B**
7. DISCOVERY MOTIONS
8. MOTION FOR SUMMARY JUDGMENT
9. MEDIATION OR SETTLEMENT CONFERENCE
10. STATUS CONFERENCE TRIAL READINESS CONFERENCE
11. TRIAL SETTING CONFERENCE
12. MEET WITH JUDGE

**C**
13. SELECT JURY
14. OPENING STATEMENT
15. PLAINTIFF'S EVIDENCE
16. DEFENDANT'S EVIDENCE
17. MOTION TO DISMISS
18. SELECT JURY INSTRUCTIONS

**D**
19. CLOSING ARGUMENT OF PLAINTIFF
20. CLOSING ARGUMENT OF DEFENDANT
21. INSTRUCT JURY
22. JURY DELIBERATION
23. JURY VERDICT
24. POST TRIAL MOTIONS

**E**
25. WINNER FILES COST BILL
26. MOTION FOR NEW TRIAL
27. FILE NOTICE OF APPEAL
28. FILE APPEAL BOND
29. FILE APPEAL AND ORDER TRANSCRIPTS OF TRIAL
30. PREPARE AND FILE APPELLATE BRIEF

**F**
31. FILE OPPOSITION BRIEF
32. FILE RESPONDING BRIEF
33. STATUS CONFERENCE
34. SETTLEMENT CONFERENCE
35. ORAL ARGUMENT
36. APPELLATE OPINION

**G**
37. PETITION FOR RE-HEARING
38. PETITION FOR HEARING TO SUPREME COURT
39. PREPARE AND FILE OPENING BRIEF
40. FILE OPPOSITION BRIEF
41. FILE RESPONDING BRIEF
42. ORAL ARGUMENT

**H**
43. COURT OPINION
44. NOTICE OF ENTRY OF JUDGMENT
45. ORDER OF EXECUTION ON JUDGMENT
46. EXECUTION ON JUDGMENT
47. NOTICE OF SATISFACTION OF JUDGMENT

# ANATOMY OF A PROFESSIONAL LIABILITY TRIAL

The timeline is included here in order for you to be aware of the complex, expensive, and very time-consuming process of a medical malpractice lawsuit, from its beginning through its final hearing in the Supreme Court. The numbered paragraphs described below explain the numbered points on the timeline set out graphically in the illustration on page 177.

1. **Notice to Defendant:** In many jurisdictions, the plaintiff must receive an expert opinion before a complaint can be filed. Notice to the defendant or defendants is given when a complaint is anticipated.

2. **Expert Opinion:** An expert in the medical specialty involving the complaint must be obtained at the outset in order to frame the pleadings and provide the attorney with valuable advice.

3. **Plaintiff Files Complaint:** This is the event that puts the cause of action in operation and triggers the time within which the defendants must respond.

4. **Defendant Attacks Complaint:** Quite often the defendants would like to test the complaint from a legal standpoint and they file a demurer or motion to dismiss, as a matter of law, and narrow the legal issues of the case.

5. **Defendant Files an Answer:** The defendant raises defenses in the answer, and in some jurisdictions, may allege an offset or a counterclaim at the same time.

6. **Discovery:** Discovery is a process by which facts, usually under oath, are "discovered" by means of depositions, testimony under oath, and interrogatories, written questions to be answered under oath, and notices to produce documents and other things that may be important to the case.

7. **Discovery Motions:** If the responding party does not respond or the response is inadequate, the propounding party may then move the court for an order compelling responses.

8. **Motion for Summary Judgment or Dismissal:** The parties may move the court for a judgment in the case but only as to issues of law. Questions of fact must be determined by the trier of fact—the jury, or if there is no jury, the court based on admissible evidence.

9. **Mediations of Settlement Conferences:** When the motions have been completed, and if they are unsuccessful and the case remains at issue, the court will order some process of informal resolution in most jurisdictions. Mediation seems to be the most successful settlement process.

10. **Status Conference and Trial Readiness Conference:** In many jurisdictions, these conferences are one and the same and merely are to motivate the parties to bring their cases into order for the court to begin the process toward setting a trial.

11. **Trial Setting Conference:** After the court determines the readiness of the case, it will set the trial for a time within the court's calendar that will accommodate the trial calendars, not only of the court but of all the counsel involved.

12. **Meet with the Judge:** After the case has been set for trial, as well as on the date of trial, counsel will meet with the judge to sort out the issues that are now going to be put before the court and the jury.

13. **Select the Jury:** In the minds of many attorneys, this is the most critical part of the trial. The jury can be informed of the nature of the case, and counsel try to pre-educate the jury members on their point of view

through voir dire, which is a very old Norman French word that means "to seek the truth." These are questions posed to the jurors regarding their backgrounds, knowledge, experience, and other aspects of their lives that may influence their decisions on the facts in the case. Each side is usually given a certain member of preemptory challenges and may thank and excuse a prospective juror without giving any reason. Certainly, if there is a reason for cause, the parties either stipulate to the excusing of the juror or the court will order it.

14. **Opening Statements:** Before any evidence is presented, the parties are given the opportunity to give an overview of what they contend the evidence will show. This is also a very important part of the case, and opening statements should rarely be waived by the attorneys because the jurors' first impressions are very important. The opening statements are not evidence.

15. **Plaintiff's Evidence:** The plaintiff has the burden of proof in a civil case in most jurisdictions, consisting of the preponderance of evidence.

16. **Defendant's Evidence:** The defendant is given the opportunity to bring forth evidence to refute the evidence of the plaintiff. Both plaintiffs and defendants can put on expert testimony within the time allotted for their presentations.

17. **Motions to Dismiss or for Nonsuit:** If a motion for a nonsuit is not made by defendant at the close of plaintiff's evidence, it may be made at this point in the trial because all of the evidence is in from the plaintiffs and the defendants.

18. **Select Jury Instructions:** The jury must be instructed by the court on the law of the case. It is the court's duty to give these instructions, and the court must seek the requested instructions on the law of the case from all parties.

19. **Closing Argument of the Plaintiff:** Unlike the opening statement in the closing statement, counsel may argue those things that have been admitted into evidence to construct theories of the case openly before the jury and ask the jury to arrive at certain conclusions based on the evidence.

20. **Closing Argument of the Defendant:** The defendant now has the opportunity to argue that the preponderance of the evidence has not been met and there should be a verdict for the defendant.

21. **Instruct the Jury:** At this time the jury instructions and the laws of the case are read by the court to the jury.

22. **Jury Deliberation:** Many trial attorneys will tell you that this is the most difficult part of the case. Waiting for the jury to make its decision can be agonizing for the parties and their counsel. Within the locked confines of the jury room, the jury elects a foreperson, examines the evidence, follows the instructions, and makes the determination of fact necessary for them to reach a verdict either for the plaintiff or the defendant.

23. **Jury Verdict:** After the deliberations have been completed, the jury arrives at a verdict.

24. **Post Trial Motions:** Even after the jury verdict has been read aloud and even after the jury has been polled—that is, each individual juror is asked if the verdict is the verdict of that individual member—there are issues that counsel for the parties must consider. Posttrial motions include motions for a new trial.

25. **Prevailing Party Files Cost Bill:** The prevailing party may be entitled to recover court costs and in some cases, attorney's fees and other costs.

26. **Motions for a New Trial:** Frequently motions for a new trial are conditioned upon such additions or reductions of the verdict. The posttrial motions can be critical and form the basis for issues on appeal if unsuccessful.

27. **File Notice of Appeal:** At this point the non-prevailing party may file a notice of appeal. Generally this has the effect of ending the jurisdiction of the trial court.

28. **File Appeal Bond:** The court can order a bond posted by the appealing party.

29. **File the Appeal and Order Transcripts of Trial:** The appellate process begins in earnest when the brief of the appealing party is filed and the court orders transcripts to be produced.

30. **Prepare and File Appellate Brief:** There are law firms whose specialty is limited to appellate work and they do nothing at the trial level, only at the appellate level.

31. **File Opposition Brief:** After receiving the appellate brief of the appealing party, the appellee has the opportunity to file an opposition brief within a certain time limit.

32. **File Responding Brief:** The appellant then must, if it decides to do so, prepare a responding brief.

33. **Status Conference:** The appellate court, like a trial court, must maintain control of its calendar and determine the status of cases that are before it.

34. **Settlement Conference:** The appellate court is just as interested in resolving cases informally as any other court. Settlement conferences, mediations, and other means of resolving the case informally are explored and may be ordered by the court.

35. **Oral Argument:** Oral argument can be made simply and powerfully and the attorneys and the judges do not get lost in a sea of written words when oral presentations can clarify them. This is also an opportunity for the court to ask counsel very pointed questions with respect to their positions in the case.

36. **The Appellate Opinion:** After hearing the argument and after a time for deliberation, the appellate court will issue a written opinion.

37. **Petition for Rehearing:** Counsel who are unsuccessful in persuading the court may make an attempt to have the court hear and consider cases that have come down in the meantime and that may have a bearing on the case.

38. **Petition for Hearing to Supreme Court:** If the petition for rehearing has been unsuccessful, the unsuccessful party may then seek a hearing in the court above the appellate court. In most jurisdictions this is the state Supreme Court. In federal jurisdiction cases, it is the U.S. Supreme Court.

39. **Prepare and File Opening Brief:** If the petition for hearing to the higher court is successful then a brief must be prepared for that court to consider.

40. **File Opposition Brief:** As in the lower appellate court sequence, the opposition brief must be filed to attack the issues raised in the opening brief.

41. **File Responding Brief:** Response to the opposition is quite brief because most of the issues have been honed and refined to the point where they are relatively clear for all concerned.

42. **Oral Argument:** In the higher court, or the Supreme Court, oral argument is made by the parties as an opportunity to clarify the issues in the case, both in the court's mind and for counsel. This is a way for observers to gauge how the court is leaning.

43. **Court Opinion:** The opinion of the court is in writing and usually isolates the issues and can set precedence to give future cases guidance on how they should be decided at the lower levels.

44. **Notice of Entry of Judgment:** The judgment is now entered against the losing party and the force of the

judicial system can be brought to bear, to execute on the assets of the party that did not prevail, either for a judgment, verdict, or for costs and other recoverable items.

45. **Order of Execution on Judgment:** The order can be used to execute on property, have a keeper placed at a business in order to impound the funds, and otherwise get the moneys necessary to satisfy the judgment.

46. **Execution on the Judgment:** After the order has been made, the process of execution is rather simple, powerful, quick, and decisive.

47. **Notice of Satisfaction of Judgment:** Such a notice indicates that the file is closed, the matter is complete, and there is no longer any necessary activity.

# MEDIATION

Since the 1980s, people involved in businesses and professions have increasingly required in their contracts the use of arbitration and mediation to resolve disputes arising out of those contracts. Appellate courts have repeatedly held that contracts requiring *alternative dispute resolution* (ADR) are valid and enforceable. Negotiation and mediation are the two processes that allow you to participate in and decide the outcome of disputes.

*Negotiation* is defined as two or more people seeking a goal by giving and receiving concessions. *Mediation* is simply defined as impartial third-party assisted negotiation. A mediator may be anyone whom the parties trust and who has the skills of a master negotiator.

In a medical context, issues can become very personal and emotional. Strong feelings can interfere with successful communication. Matters are only worsened if people are forced into litigation. Professional help through mediation may save a great deal of expense and vexation. A few guidelines for negotiating can be helpful in any conflict.

- Have all of the relevant facts before entering the process. Do your homework.
- Successful mediation involves compromise on the part of all of the parties. Determine how much you are willing to concede.
- Enter the process with an open mind. Unrealistic expectations, take-it-or-leave-it offers, lack of preparation, and strident adversarial attitudes doom mediations before they begin.
- Listen. You may wish to set ground rules for the length of time each speaker can hold the floor. When someone is speaking, give your full attention.
- Make a determined effort to be aware of others' feelings. Put yourself in their position and imagine how you would feel and react.
- Maintain a pleasant demeanor. Overly aggressive advocacy has its place, but not in negotiation or mediation. You should maintain a strong position, but not an oppressive one.
- If possible, let your opponent make the opening offer. If you must make the first offer, it should: (1) send a signal that you are interested in resolving the problem by being reasonable; (2) give the other side something to think about but leave you room for alternative offers later; and (3) contain additional points that you are willing to concede, depending on the counteroffer.
- If you give up too soon, you are likely to lose to those more tenacious than you. Always have a counterproposal to keep the door open.

Mediation is the method of choice to resolve disputes. It can be initiated at any stage of the proceedings, and interrupted and resumed at any time. All sides generally benefit from mediation, and a successful mediation results in all sides feeling quite satisfied with the result. Successful mediation must lead to a written agreement.

To participate in mediation, it is necessary to include the people who make the final decision as well as those who have critical knowledge of the matters in dispute. A positive tone must be maintained by all parties.

Although mediation is generally considered a process whereby only one mediator is used, another process has been developed by the Rush Medical Center in Chicago, Illinois (formally known as Rush University Medical Center). The Rush Medical Center developed a mediation format whereby the plaintiff's counsel in a medical malpractice lawsuit is given the option of choosing a single mediator, retired judge, or co-mediators—one an experienced medical malpractice plaintiff's counsel and the other an experienced medical malpractice defense counsel.

The program is sponsored by Rush and the parties share the expenses equally. By giving the plaintiff the option of the style of mediation and the choice of mediators, Rush has successfully demonstrated that they are sincere in their efforts to bring cases to resolution and to rid the plaintiffs of the fears that bias in the system will be against them.

Statistically, the success of the Rush system is quite remarkable. The co-mediator style is generally preferred, with the success rate of their cases in excess of 85%. The cases were resolved generally within three to four hours. The defense costs, as well as those for the plaintiffs, are greatly reduced, and the satisfaction of both sides is very high in almost all cases.

Mediation generally, and the Rush model in particular, gives the hospital administrator or the insurance representative more direct control over how the matter is to be handled in its final stages. The feeling of participation by both sides is part of the reason for the success, and the personal satisfaction of participating in one's own destiny is another positive factor.

The Rush model has not yet been adopted in many jurisdictions, and the co-mediation aspect may be one of the reasons. The prevalence of mediation, however, is increasing and the choice of arbitration is on the decline.

# ARBITRATION

*Arbitration* is essentially a trial without a jury, without a written record, and with very relaxed rules of evidence. Many people do not know the difference between mediation and arbitration. Arbitration can be extremely harsh, and in many jurisdictions there is no appeal from the award even though the arbitrator or arbitrators may be wrong on the facts and the law. As arbitration has become used more and more, it becomes increasingly expensive because both sides want to have discovery, expert witnesses, and other aspects of a trial, and so the expenses approach those of an actual trial.

Mediation is completely different from arbitration. The mediator takes no evidence in a formal proceeding and makes no award or other formal decision. The parties and their lawyers resolve their dispute. With arbitration, a third-party stranger makes the decisions.

In an arbitration there is no settlement. The arbitration results in an award. It is enforceable when a court confirms the award as a judgment. Binding arbitration is true litigation—although the rules of evidence may be relaxed, someone has to lose. There may be either a single arbitrator or a panel of three arbitrators, and their expenses are shared equally by the parties. The advantages are that the process is fast, fair, and final.

Testimony under oath is required in arbitration, although there may be no written record of the proceedings. This has a sobering effect on most witnesses and motivates many people to negotiate their disputes.

The recovery of attorney's fees, which can be very large, also motivates the parties to negotiate a resolution. If a physician stubbornly refuses to admit a mistake, even in the face of convincing evidence, the costs of arbitration may encourage mediation.

## ADR TRAINING FOR PHYSICIANS

This book is not the place for a complete course for *alternative dispute resolution* (ADR). All people involved in the health care professions should be training in how to participate in ADR as witnesses or parties. For example, mediation is defined as "impartial, third-party assisted negotiation." Therefore, training in negotiation is essential to a positive settlement.

Arbitration is completely the opposite. A stranger or strangers make the decision for the parties just as a judge does, only there is no transcript and limited appeal grounds. The matter is concluded by an award, not a settlement.

Increasingly, hospitals are using mediation as well as arbitration requirements in their contracts with physicians, patients, and vendors. Similarly, physicians are requiring such agreements with their patients, before treatments begin. Your liability carrier and your professional associations will have suggested forms available for you to use. Most courts have upheld the validity of contracts, which make ADR a condition of providing medical services.

Many hospitals are beginning to use teams to handle errors in medical treatment. These teams may include risk managers, hospital executives, nursing managers, physicians, ethicists, mediators, and negotiators.

Training for ADR is going to become more and more necessary as dispute resolution generally becomes a part of the professional activities of physicians. For example, there are conflicts between physician and patient, physician and patients' families, physician and staff, physician and physician, and physician and administrators, HMOs and insurance companies, among other possible disputes.

Seminars, classrooms, workshops and other modes of ADR training are less effective, it would seem, for medical practitioners than the mentoring style. Participation in role playing, or at least observing actual or role-played mediations in progress, allows students to be mentored as they see people in mediation, negotiation, or even arbitration.

In negotiation, no third party is necessary and the expense can be kept at a minimum. Additionally, such disputes may not carry any of the enormous financial consequences of those between physician and patient or patients' families.

Role playing is the optimum teaching method for negotiation and it can be extremely valuable for your practice to involve the new or newest physicians in the negotiation process when dealing with vendors, staff, or anyone else with whom you have even a good-natured conflict in a business context.

When you find yourself involved in a lawsuit or an arbitration involving multiple defendants, such as other physicians and health care practitioners and hospitals, you may want to suggest to your legal counsel that the negotiations, or more importantly, the mediation, begin with a session involving only the defendants in order for such things as coverage issues, indemnification issues, and other things that do not directly affect the plaintiff can be resolved and the defendants face the plaintiff in negotiation or mediation with a more united front.

# chapter fifteen:
# Preventing Malpractice Suits

You can do a lot to avoid malpractice claims or other complaints about your medical care. The most controllable factor is the quality of your relationship with your patients. In many cases, it is the physician's attitude that is the chief cause for action against the physician. Indifference, arrogance, or anger can trigger such a lawsuit. You hear stories of surgeons throwing instruments across the operating room, and physicians stalking out of examining rooms or getting into arguments with patients or members of their families. These behaviors trigger lawsuits by patients and their families.

Doctors' and managers' time and resources are engaged more and more in the resolution of complaints and claims, whether justified or not, especially today, with so many medical plans in use. Doctors targeted by malpractice suits can expect to experience increased stress, anger, frustration, mood changes, irritability, depression, and physical complaints, including headaches and insomnia. These are in addition to the drain on their time and money, and the disruption of their practice.

A malpractice suit is a serious event. When you are starting out in your practice, you should not be naïve, but should be well aware of the seriousness of such an action, and do everything within your power to prevent and avoid it.

The size of your practice or your group will dictate the procedures that you undertake to deal with risk management. If your group is large you may even have an individual in the group whose role is to handle risk management issues. A sole practitioner or small group practice has the same exposure to liability, but may not need the expense and the overhead of a professional risk manager. In those cases, consultants or business management groups can be engaged to conduct your risk management needs on an outsourcing basis. This will be more cost effective for you.

In medical malpractice suits, physicians typically are certain of their rights and are often challenged by the necessity of apologies. When conflicts arise, a simple apology may ease tensions and even reduce the possibility of a lawsuit.

## CONFRONTING THE UNEXPECTED OUTCOME

There are many reasons why the outcome of a treatment or procedure could be unexpected. In some cases there could be physician error; in other cases, accident. The doctor may have deviated from the standard of care. There may be unexpected complications in the procedure or the patient's health status that interfere with the desired outcome. In many cases, while the doctor may feel that the results are as good as could be expected, the patient, or the patient's family, may have unreasonably optimistic expectations, so that anything short of a miraculous cure would be disappointing.

Whatever the reason, whatever the causes, and wherever the actual or perceived fault lies, unexpected outcomes must be discussed. The best time to begin this discussion is before the treatment or procedure. The more complex the diagnosis and treatment, the more difficult this conversation can be, for both doctor and patient. The doctor, wanting the patient to provide informed consent so that the treatment can proceed, may be reluctant to scare off the patient by describing every possible complication. The patient, perhaps confronting his or her own fragility or mortality for the first time, may not be able to absorb the doctor's explanations.

This conversation should include information about the procedure, complications, prognosis for healing, and realistic expectations for the short- and long-term. Patients should have the opportunity to bring a family member into the discussion. They should also, if time allows, be offered a follow-up conversation, after they have time to absorb the information provided and to come up with additional questions. The physician should make every effort to avoid rushing through the discussion, and always ask confirming questions to assure that the patient understands. The desired result of this conversation is that the patient will feel greater trust for the doctor and will be an active participant in decision making about his or her own care.

When the treatment or procedure has resulted in an adverse outcome—even if there has been such a pretreatment discussion—the doctor must quickly and carefully address the relevant issues with the patient and/or the patient's family. You must decide whether this subject should be discussed with your liability carrier before you go to the patient or patient's family. While a doctor's first impulse may be to avoid a discussion in order to avoid a malpractice suit, doctors must discuss with their patients "the outcomes of care that differ significantly from anticipated outcomes," according to the Joint Commission on Accreditation of Healthcare Organizations (JCAHO). This is, by nature, a difficult conversation. There are several points to remember.

- **Do not delay.** Delays may not only cause the patient to feel that he or she is being deceived or that the doctor does not care, but also rapid disclosure may allow interventions that can reduce the negative effect of the outcome.
- **Select a private place for the conversation.** Conducting this conversation in the hospital hallway or waiting room is disrespectful, and the doctor will be perceived as indifferent or uncaring. Such perceptions contribute measurably to an individual's decision to sue for malpractice.
- **Express care and avoid defensiveness.** Patients and family members may be upset and angry, and may directly challenge the physician. Even if you are feeling defensive, carefully avoid language that may be interpreted as defensive. Answer one question at a time. Use straightforward, nontechnical language. Repeat explanations as necessary. Throughout the conversation, express concern and care about the patient's well-being.
- **Be honest.** Explain what happened and admit mistakes. Apologize. Avoid casting blame on others—including the patient.

Your office staff can be extremely helpful in making patients feel more secure with the treatment they receive. By using appropriate language, demonstrating respect and caring, and assuring that disclosure forms are understood and signed, well-trained staff encourage patients to trust the practice and to participate in decisions about their care. Even if there is physician error, doctors who discuss outcomes honestly, directly, empathetically, and in a timely fashion have a far lower incidence of malpractice suits.

# THE HEALING VALUE OF "I'M SORRY"

You are late for an appointment, or you have kept a patient waiting. You have forgotten to return a phone call, or to send a colleague the documents or test results you promised. So what do you do? Perhaps you act as if nothing has happened—you are a busy professional after all—or maybe you issue a breezy apology and then act as if nothing has happened.

If you do not mention your lapse, your patient or colleague will see you as either scatterbrained or arrogant. If your apology is thoughtless or cursory, you will be perceived as insincere. In neither case does the other party feel any better, and your professional status is weakened.

Remember, *these apology guidelines are for minor matters, not potential medical malpractice.* After malpractice claims are settled, your legal counsel may advise you on whether an apology for such a claim is permitted.

The fact is, we all make mistakes. We forget things. We are late. We break promises. Try as we might to keep our lives in order, such lapses are inevitable. Doctors' lapses can have serious personal and economic consequences—for their patients and for themselves.

Perfectionists by nature, doctors are trained to be superhuman in order to avoid mistakes. With high expectations, they may see an apology as not only a bothersome social convention, but also an admission of fallibility. They may have a tendency to blame circumstances or other people rather than admit they have some responsibility for the problem.

While medical school training may have included warnings against apologies as actionable admissions of responsibility, studies indicate that apologies are a powerful tool in diffusing a patient's anger, restoring respect, and actually reducing the number of complaints that end up in malpractice suits.

Like all of the other tools that doctors use, apologies require practice and skill before they can be added to the healing regimen. Here are some apology guidelines to start that process.

- Acknowledge that there is a problem. Before you can find a solution, you need to admit that there is a problem and begin to define it.
- Admit to yourself that you may have some responsibility for the problem. Even if you think you have absolutely no responsibility, an apology may still be in order.
- Put yourself in the other party's position. Whether it is a colleague or a patient, how is he or she affected by the problem? Consider how his or her life may have been disrupted and how the problem may in turn have further repercussions for his or her work, family, finances, or future.
- Find out what information the other party needs. In most cases, people want to know what happened and why, what the effects and costs will be, and how the problem can be avoided in the future.
- Do not procrastinate. The longer you wait to confront the issue, the more of a problem it will be.
- Make time to apologize. An effective apology is a conversation, not a speech. Allow time for a complete exchange.
- Apologize. If you are able to apologize in person, which is always the best choice, make eye contact. Tell the person you are sorry. Acknowledge that he or she may have been inconvenienced or damaged by something you did. Explain what happened, but avoid blaming and making excuses. Provide the information the other person needs. Ask for his or her response.

- Listen. Allow the other party to express him- or herself completely. Especially if the party is angry, he or she may want to go back to the beginning, restate the problem, and find blame. Be patient and avoid being defensive. Express your understanding and appreciation for the other party's pain and anger.
- Avoid interruptions. Do not interrupt the other person while he or she is talking. Also, arrange a time and place for your conversation where you will not be interrupted by people, phones, or other scheduled commitments.
- Agree on a solution. Find something that gives everyone involved at least some satisfaction. Even if you still believe you are not wrong, you may have to compromise in order to find a solution. The more serious the problem, the longer this may take.

If you have analyzed the problem frankly and you believe you have no responsibility for it, you may still be able to use an apology to express your concern and empathy for the other person. This may have the beneficial effect of making you seem more caring, bringing about better doctor/patient relations, and possibly leading to a productive conversation that will help the person find a solution.

Every contact you have—whether it is with a patient, an office or hospital staff person, another physician, or a friend or family member—is a relationship. Healthy relationships require honesty, nurturing, listening, trust, and mutual respect. In case after case, patients who pursue malpractice suits cite their doctor's lack of respect and empathy as contributing factors in their decision to pursue litigation. Difficult as it may seem, apologizing is a tremendously effective indicator of honesty and respect, and an important step in restoring trust.

# CLEAR COMMUNICATIONS FOR HEALTHY OUTCOMES

The way that physicians communicate with their patients has a direct impact on patient satisfaction and may actually reduce the likelihood of malpractice suits. In today's highly litigious society, healing the patient is a most desirable result of treatment, but not the only one. Physicians also need to do everything possible to protect themselves against lawsuits.

The pressures on doctors are enormous—time is short, financial burdens ever-increasing, and the need to stay current on new data and procedures never ending. There may be little time for reflection or spiritual growth, family interaction, exercise, healthy diet, or recreation. Physicians may feel that they are racing from patient to patient, commitment to commitment, all day, every day. It is easy to think that there is simply no time for a caring bedside manner.

Before rushing through another appointment, consider these important ideas.

- Patients want to feel that their doctors care about them. One of the best ways to demonstrate care and compassion is to ask questions and listen carefully to the answers.
- A doctor who is multitasking—thinking about his or her last patient, debts, or golf game while meeting with a patient—is not communicating effectively.
- Patients value ongoing relationships with their doctors. They expect their doctors to remember them, be familiar with their medical concerns, and ask appropriate questions. A few personal notes in a patient's file may trigger valuable recollections for a busy physician.
- Having to wait excessive lengths of time to see a doctor is offensive to patients. It shows a lack of respect for patients' time, especially if it happens on every visit. While

occasional delays are unavoidable, good time management is part of effective patient care. Apologize if the patient had to wait. If this is a chronic problem, find a solution. One approach is to call patients if the doctor is running more than thirty minutes behind; another is to have the receptionist inform patients about wait times when they arrive; yet another is to post a white board at the reception desk with each doctor's name and the current wait times. While on-time appointments should be every doctor's goal, keeping patients informed shows respect and reduces resentment; if a patient knows he or she will have to wait, he or she may be able to manage his or her own time—make a phone call, get a cup of coffee, run an errand—while waiting.

- Patient education contributes to good medical results and perceived physician caring. Take the time to explain procedures and possible outcomes, answer questions, and help the patient secure more information.
- Confirm understanding by repeating statements and asking additional questions.
- A follow-up phone call after an outpatient procedure goes a long way toward demonstrating physician care.
- Given identical outcomes, patients are more likely to sue a doctor that seems uncaring than they are one who demonstrates interest and care.

Let patients know you care. Treat them as human beings, not as things to be worked on. Take some interest in patients' personal lives by asking questions about their families or vacation plans. Even a frightened or disgruntled patient can melt when asked to talk about the grandchildren.

Patients are like customers in any other business. They want quality service, reasonable fees, open communication, and the feeling that you are taking good care of them. Rendering quality care, keeping up with advances in your field, and sharpening your medical skills constantly will show through in your discussions with patients and their families.

Effective interpersonal communication is a learned skill. It does not mean that meetings with patients have to drag on through endless conversations, but rather that both doctor and patient are focused on the patient's concerns at each meeting. When physicians improve their listening and speaking skills, they provide better care for their patients—and themselves!

# MANAGING RISK AND REDUCING LIABILITY

*Lawsuit.* The word is enough to raise your pulse and bring on waves of anxiety. The reality is capable of seriously disrupting or even ending careers, ruining reputations, or at the least, adding long-term financial stress to personal and professional lives. With such dire consequences, it makes sense to start reducing the risk of lawsuits immediately. Certainly, as you establish your new practice, thorough and thoughtful risk management procedures should be put in place that can be followed easily, whatever the size of your practice.

Although some malpractice suits are based on a single act, most are influenced by a wide range of factors, from the profession-alism of your front office staff to the cleanliness of your restrooms and the promptness of returned phone calls. An effective risk management policy takes in all the potential areas of concern and actually makes your practice more professional and congenial for patients and staff.

Your risk management policies must go far beyond the purchase of malpractice insurance, although your insurance carrier may be able to provide some additional useful guidelines. Written, comprehensive risk management policies form an essential core of your office procedures manual and a vital element of staff and physician training.

You can demonstrate your respect for your patients and their opinions by preparing and distributing a patient feedback form or satisfaction survey. (see page 209.) Ask for comments and suggestions. When a patient suggestion is implemented, make a special effort to say thank you to the patient who provided it.

In establishing your risk management practices, it is helpful to take the perspective of a patient. What does the patient see and experience in his or her interactions with you and your office? First impressions are difficult to counteract, so make every effort to assure that the first impression is a good one. Remember— the doctor sets the tone. If you treat your staff and patients with genuine warmth and respect, they are far more likely to respect you—and less likely to sue you—in return.

# Checklist for Developing a Risk Management Policy

Use this checklist to be certain that vital areas of your practice are included as you develop your risk management policy. Each topic should include detailed protocols, including who is responsible, how often, what documentation is required, how that documentation will be maintained, and how you will assure that the policies are followed. As you update your policy, make sure that the revision date appears on every page.

**Waiting area**
- ❏ Who is responsible for music, furnishings, artwork, lighting, and what approvals are required for change
- ❏ Detail what will be offered, such as magazines, informational brochures, coffee/tea, and who keeps it stocked
- ❏ Who maintains plants or fish tank
- ❏ Who is responsible for maintenance, including checking condition of upholstery, carpeting, and other surfaces, and how often

**Patient admitting**
- ❏ Sign-in procedures
- ❏ Staff introductions
- ❏ Record updates
- ❏ Wait times

**Office staff**
- ❏ Telephone and office etiquette
- ❏ Management of frequently asked questions
- ❏ Confidentiality
- ❏ Training—including first aid, CPR, and equipment
- ❏ Appropriate licensure
- ❏ Empathy
- ❏ Staff meetings
- ❏ Attire, including name badges and use of perfume

**Office staff area**
- ❏ Phone and conversation volume and confidentiality
- ❏ Personal items in office
- ❏ Eating in office
- ❏ Bulletin boards
- ❏ Flowers

**Day of visit information**
- ❏ Preferred terms of address for doctor, staff, and patients
- ❏ Allergies
- ❏ Reason for visit
- ❏ Current prescriptions
- ❏ Recent diagnoses
- ❏ Recent test results or consults from other physicians

## Examination rooms
❑ Wait times
❑ Privacy and modesty
❑ Chaperone presence
❑ Cleanliness, hand-washing, infection control
❑ Safety

## Other patient-accessible areas
❑ Restrooms
❑ Hallways
❑ Radiation and other treatment rooms
❑ Cleanliness
❑ Appropriate warning signs
❑ Appropriate waiting areas where patients can be safe and comfortable, out of the way of office staff, and unlikely to see or overhear other patients or their files

## Other areas of office
❑ Storage areas
❑ Lab areas and equipment
❑ Files

## Patient/doctor contact
❑ Terms of address
❑ Review of medical records
❑ Gaining consent and documentation of consent
❑ Listening
❑ Diagnoses, including policy regarding phone/fax/email/in-person delivery of diagnoses
❑ Recommendations
❑ Procedures to assure staff follow-through on doctor's orders

## Special situations
❑ In-office emergencies
❑ Dealing with medical errors
❑ Interpreters
❑ Patients who need physical assistance
❑ High-risk patients
❑ Incompetent patients
❑ State or locally required reporting of illness or abuse

## Recordkeeping
❑ System
❑ Method of recording information
❑ Proofreading and double-checking chart entries
❑ Method of integrating paper files into electronic system and disposition of paper files thereafter
❑ Method of correcting errors or late entries
❑ Special coding

❏ Methods of sharing patient information, including requests for patient records from other physicians
❏ Providing record access to patient
❏ Maintenance, backup, and archiving of paper and electronic records

**Other communications**
❏ Confidentiality of shared information
❏ Reporting test results
❏ Documenting telephone conversations and messages

**Handling complaints**
❏ In-person, phone, and written procedures
❏ Who handles
❏ Documentation
❏ Assuring follow-up
❏ Use of patient satisfaction survey

**Scheduling issues**
❏ Making appointments
❏ Reminders
❏ Late arrivals
❏ Missed appointments
❏ Chronically late patients
❏ Doctor emergencies that require schedule changes

**Billing issues**
❏ Billing and insurance protocols
❏ Handling late payments
❏ Handling disputes
❏ Sending accounts to collection

**Educational materials**
❏ Types of materials available
❏ Where and how distributed
❏ Documentation of receipt, if appropriate

**Other office practices**
❏ Reviewing test results prior to filing
❏ Approval of prescription refill requests
❏ Safety shields
❏ Laboratory logging
❏ Sterilization procedures
❏ Vacation scheduling for doctor and staff
❏ Referrals to other physicians and services
❏ Protocols, notifications, forwarding of files

**After-hours services and policies**
❏ Answering service
❏ Night phone message
❏ Rotation of on-call

# ADDITIONAL SUGGESTIONS FOR RISK MANAGEMENT

In addition to establishing good office policies, there are additional measures you can take for risk management. For example, buy insurance. A few doctors feel that they are not vulnerable to malpractice suits, so they fail to buy appropriate insurance. This is a mistake. Anyone can be sued—regardless of their specialty, years in business, or practice size.

Screen your patients carefully. You want all the business you can get, but it is important to take the time to evaluate new patients. If a potential patient has a history of lawsuits, of firing or speaking badly of their doctors, or of being turned down by other doctors, be extremely cautious. If you have a bad feeling about a potential patient, trust your instincts.

Discuss expectations. Your patients may have an unclear or unrealistic view of what will happen in the course of treatment. They may not understand that you cannot make their body perfect again. Their expectations may be based on sensational newspaper coverage or television dramatizations. Explain the process clearly before you begin treatment and review the progress regularly as you move forward. Encourage your patients to express their concerns and their acknowledgment during these conversations.

Expectations and roles should be clarified in your charting to assure that both patient and doctor understand their mutual responsibilities, and what roles other consultants may play in getting them well. Be as specific as possible in naming the exact scope of your responsibilities.

Everyone makes mistakes. The worst possible way to deal with a mistake is to ignore it. Seek advice from experienced advisors, especially your medical malpractice company representative. Provide whatever information the patient needs and offer a solution. Ask for feedback and listen carefully to the response.

Attend to all of your patients. One patient's complex medical problem may be claiming your interest and attention, but do not ignore the routine or more difficult patients. The ones you ignore are the ones who are most likely to sue you.

Keep track of a patient's ongoing treatment. The number one cause of medical malpractice cases is lack of proper follow-up. Pay attention to laboratory results, referrals, and the progress of patients returning for follow-up treatment. Communicate with the physicians who cover for you and those for whom you cover.

Staff meetings, which are essential for sharing information, correcting problems, and building morale, should be scheduled regularly—once a week at least—with attendance mandatory. Choose a time when you are least likely to be interrupted, such as the half-hour before the office opens in the morning. The information that is shared at these meetings is an important part of your risk-management strategy. With open communication channels in the office, well-managed meetings do not need to take more than fifteen to thirty minutes. A checklist for conducting meetings appears on page 211.

Take care of yourself. You are more vulnerable to malpractice suits if you are unable to manage your work due to stress. Eat regular meals, take breaks, get some exercise, and take regular vacations. A doctor who takes no vacation is dangerous to patients, the staff, and him- or herself.

Use the best diagnostic methods and procedures available. Document differential diagnoses and indicate your reasons for discarding all but the primary one. Review all laboratory reports and X-rays, and comment upon them in your notes.

If your risk and your insurance rates are excessive, consider reducing the number of procedures you perform. For example, if you are in general or family practice, consider giving up certain surgical procedures or even giving up surgery entirely. If you are in ob-gyn, think about discontinuing obstetrics.

Be diligent about recordkeeping. Record the facts that clearly show what your findings and actions were at the time. Whether you keep records by hand or electronically, establish and follow a protocol for making entries and corrections. Double-check everything that has been entered in a patient's record, whether it is dictated, typed, or written—and whether you see the patient in your office, at a clinic, or in the hospital.

Take an active role in your hospital staff functions and quality assurance system. If there is an error in a patient's care, you can be held accountable if you participate in that patient's care, even if someone else made the mistake.

If possible, avoid treating patients over the telephone. Although limited follow-up advice may be given if the patient was recently seen and is reliable, no new diagnoses should be made or treatment instituted. Always document each telephone call in the chart.

Try to make your office as accident-proof as possible and see that all the equipment in your office is functioning properly. Go through your office from time to time and imagine worst-case scenarios such as people falling against sharp corners, furniture tipping over, or infirm patients slipping. Correct any hazardous conditions. Have your assistants routinely help patients on and off examining tables.

Make certain that there are adequate emergency procedures established in your office manual. You should also see that your emergency equipment is up to date and complete, and that your staff holds regular drills. Be especially prepared for the added risks associated with treatments you provide, such as anesthesia.

Advise your patients of both the intended effect and any side effects that may occur from the medications you prescribe. Use AMA drug information sheets or photocopies of the pertinent pages of patient information books. Explain the side effects to the patient as you make notes. Document that you did so in the chart. Be alert for side effects and care for them properly when they occur.

Please note that these precautions do not include practicing *defensive medicine* by ordering unnecessary laboratory work, X-rays, or other procedures. This only increases the expense, not the quality of care.

# Patient Satisfaction Questionnaire

Please tell us about your visit on _____, 20_____
with Dr. _____.

|                                                                                          | YES   | NO    |
| ---------------------------------------------------------------------------------------- | ----- | ----- |
| Did you feel that you were cared about personally?                                       | _____ | _____ |
| Did you have a chance to ask questions?                                                  | _____ | _____ |
| Were medical decisions or prescriptions explained to you?                                | _____ | _____ |
| Do you now feel more confident in dealing with your medical problem?                     | _____ | _____ |
| Did you have a good experience with office staff?                                        | _____ | _____ |
| Was the waiting area pleasant and comfortable for you?                                   | _____ | _____ |
| Did you feel that you had to wait too long to see your doctor?                           | _____ | _____ |
| Was there respect given for your privacy and your special needs?                         | _____ | _____ |
| Did you feel that there was good communication between the doctor and the medical staff? | _____ | _____ |
| Did you receive prompt access to the doctor's office for information and an appointment?  | _____ | _____ |

Please add your personal comments:

_____

_____

_____

_____

_____

_____

_____

_____

_____

Thank you for helping us by providing your responses. Your care and comfort are important to us. Please be assured that we are working hard to give you the best medical care that we can.

# Checklist for Conducting Meetings

❏ Prior to the meeting, invite participants to contribute agenda items.

❏ Always have an agenda, even if it is a single-item meeting.

❏ Set a beginning and ending time, and then begin and end precisely on time.

❏ One person must be in charge of the entire meeting, even though the management of the meeting may be temporarily delegated to others for reports.

❏ Make certain that every person at the meeting has an opportunity to ask questions, make comments, or contribute to the subject of the meeting.

❏ Except for emergency issues, new or unrelated matters that are not on the agenda should be tabled and considered for the next meeting.

❏ If someone attending the meeting is disruptive or causing problems, temporarily adjourn the meeting in order for tempers to cool and disruptive people to be taken away or otherwise dealt with, then resume the meeting.

❏ If possible, keep written handouts to a minimum, and ensure the materials are relatively easy to read and digest.

❏ If the meeting agenda deals with materials that have been distributed to the attendees before the meeting, all issues and questions pertaining to that material should be addressed in the time allotted for the meeting.

# MEDICAL BOARD COMMENTS FOR PHYSICIANS

Many physicians think of lawsuits and medical board investigations as things that are unlikely to touch their lives or careers, but to be unaware of this side of the medical business is naïve. The professional consequences of such actions can be devastating, and it is important for doctors to understand how the medical board operates and some of the current trends in board investigations.

The medical board has professional oversight of a physician's career. The board's requests, communications, and actions must be taken seriously and handled promptly. When doctors receive any notice from the medical board, they must immediately obtain knowledgeable legal help and should not talk to anyone without expert advice.

The medical board becomes involved as an investigative, and potentially disciplinary, agency in all complaints against physicians. Such complaints may be about medical concerns, such as complications or poor outcomes, but today they are just as likely to involve fee disputes or inadequate communications. Unfortunately, some complaints are justified, but others may be encouraged by overzealous prosecutors. Physician discipline by the medical board is usually in two main categories: below-standard quality of care for patients and physician misconduct.

The medical board is working on improving appropriate oversight and effective prioritization of cases. Board investigators are asking complainants for more documentation and completeness regarding allegations about physicians.

Once a complaint has been filed, the process of investigation, review, and resolution can be long, costly, and disruptive. A shortage of expert reviewers may lengthen case evaluation and decisions. In addition, the medical board may require the doctor to pay *cost recovery* for costs incurred by the board during the investigation.

A doctor's role goes far beyond healing. Today's physicians must also operate well-managed businesses; maintain detailed, up-to-date medical records on every patient; establish and practice effective communication with patients and staff; and, stay current on medical and technological resources and trends. These are great demands, but well worth the effort. They can help defend a physician in the unlikely event of a medical board investigation.

# AVOIDING COMMON MEDICAL PRACTICE MISTAKES

You have devoted many years and thousands of dollars to your medical career. You are skilled and knowledgeable, and are devoted to your patients. Nonetheless, you could find your practice at risk because of simple mistakes that physicians often make in the business of medicine.

As you establish and build your medical practice, be particularly aware of these potentially devastating mistakes. Some can lead to embarrassment, some to lost patients, and some to lost careers. Following are twenty-two ways to avoid common mistakes, in order of importance.

1.  Maintain sufficient communication with the patient and others involved in patient care. This includes both any communication at all and adequate communication. Make sure that you always ask, "Do you have any questions about what I've said or the terms that I've used?" Establish a system for informing other caregivers about concerns, progress, and changes in the patient's condition and care.

2. Always return phone calls and otherwise be available to patients.

3. Do not allow inappropriate delays in triage, evaluation, treatment, and follow-up with your patient's condition.

4. Have respect for patients and staff. Respect is not a single, universally understood term. Different people have different expectations. Listening, addressing people appropriately, and not talking down to people are essential components of respect.

5. Do not make unrealistic promises. This can relate to potential outcomes of patient care as well as to your own personal and professional time commitments.

6. Master good time management, and do not keep patients waiting too long.

7. Maintain adequate on-call coverage.

8. Always explain the positive and negative outcomes of a procedure sufficiently for the patient to make informed consent.

9. Refer to a specialist for additional consultation.

10. Keep sufficient documentation in the patient's medical records of your thinking about conditions and treatments. (You may believe that you will remember what you were thinking, but you probably will not. Also, if your patient decides to move to another physician, that doctor needs to know what contributed to your decisions about the patient's care. Furthermore, patient records stand on their own in court; you will not have a chance to explain what is missing from the notes.)

11. Always proofread charts and correct typographical errors.

12. Do not practice outside of your specialty and training.

13. Do not inappropriately delegate tasks to other physicians or nonphysicians.

14. Do not prescribe medication contraindicated for the medical condition.

15. Do not use experimental or unapproved techniques or devices.

16. Keep up with technology.

17. Do not practice with uninsured physicians or other health professionals.

18. Maintain appropriate physician/patient boundaries, such as  avoiding sexual or financial involvements.

19. Do not engage in substance abuse or other unprofessional conduct.

20. Be aware of the seriousness of patient or medical board complaints.

21. Make a timely and complete disclosure of an unanticipated outcome or medical error.

22. If sued, fully prepare and cooperate appropriately with the defense team.

The attention you give to your patients needs to be complemented by equal attention to your business. Take steps as early as possible to establish systems that will keep your business running smoothly. Never ignore a small problem thinking that it will go away. At the first sign of a problem, take action to set things right. Many career catastrophes could have been prevented if the physician had admitted the mistake, with legal consultation, as soon as it occurred.

# chapter sixteen:
# Prescription for the Doctor

Perhaps you have known since age 6 that you wanted to be a doctor and never departed from that goal. Maybe career expectations were bestowed upon you by your family along with your name, or you may have come to your choice later, having tried other professions. However you arrived at medicine, you will ultimately measure your success by the achievement of goals. While timely loan, car, and mortgage payments may seem to be the only real concern, your professional goals are probably more fundamental and complex. In order to manage your career, you have to keep an eye on why you are here.

Prioritize your goals according to their current importance to you. Some possible goals you may have include autonomy, desirable location, financial reward, intellectual stimulation, job security, leisure time, personal growth, person-to-person contact, power, professional recognition, social service, and variety.

Understanding your goals allows you to set additional priorities, create timelines, and make compromises—all steps in the management of stress. Your priorities may change, so set a time each year, such as your birthday, to reconsider and reorder your list. Make sure you are still on the right track and adjust your direction accordingly.

# DIAGNOSING THE DOCTOR

The stresses heaped upon today's doctors are almost unimaginable. From an individual's first decision to enter medical training through the training itself and well into the professional career, the pressures, demands, and expectations on a physician are unrelenting. Under this burden, doctors may suffer various types and levels of impairment that can interfere with their ability to provide patient care; to interact effectively with their patients, colleagues, and family; or, to participate in the continuing education that is essential to professional development.

*Physician impairment* is not a single, easily identifiable condition. It is unique to the individual and filled with ambiguity. However, the syndrome of impaired physician is so common—the American Medical Association (AMA) estimates that one in ten allopathic physicians is impaired—that a doctor with impaired physician syndrome has been defined by the AMA as "one who is unable to practice medicine with reasonable skill and safety to patients because of physical or mental illness, including deterioration through the aging process or loss of motor skill, or excessive use or abuse of drugs including alcohol."

The Resident Physician's Section of the AMA identifies three types of impaired physician: the incompetent, the malicious or unethical, and the mentally disturbed. Malpractice profiles and state board disciplinary materials offer two further categories: the marginal and the outlier. These latter types of physicians practice medicine independent of peer feedback, without continuing education, in a manner uncommon or unreasonable in the local community (marginal), or unethical or incompetent and thereby sustaining unusually high numbers of malpractice suits (outlier).

The conditions that lead to impairment are as complex as the results. Doctors are idealized by their patients, their families, and their culture. They are not expected to have weaknesses or to become ill, are reluctant to admit illness or impairment, and in the unlikely event they should become ill, are expected to be ideal patients, able to self-heal. In addition, the medical culture tends to favor technical, scientific, and chemical solutions over human and clinical ones—facts over feelings—and doctors are slow to seek counseling or other forms of compassionate support.

Such high expectations can lead to perfectionist behavior, overidentification with their role as doctors, and denial of their own humanness. There is an intense fear of failure: *I am a doctor. If I fail to meet these expectations, I am nothing.*

The demands for superior achievement begin in the premed years, when students compete fiercely and sacrifice the breadth of their academic and social experience to focus on the achievements that will show on their transcripts. While some students may enter their medical training already suffering from related problems, impairment often begins during medical training, continues during residency, and persists into the pro-fessional practice. Training is typically structured as a total immersion—a brutal test of ability and endurance—that neglects sleep, regular meals, social interaction, and familial support in the name of professional achievement. While doctors are trained to provide holistic treatment for their patients, they learn to ignore themselves as whole persons. Opportunities for support, rest, or time for reflection or recreation are always at the bottom of the list. Professional demands prevail over personal needs.

Impaired physicians seldom see their own distress or take it seriously, and in general, continue with their practices. They are slow to seek treatment, resistant to help, and reluctant to follow a course of recommended treatment.

The impact of impairment may affect every aspect of a doctor's personal and professional life, including his or her decisions, diagnoses, and communications. It can lead to mistakes, impaired judgment, burnout, and a higher risk of chemical dependency, mental illness, depression, and suicide.

The solution to physician impairment depends upon early recognition; changes to medical training protocols, including the common training model, which is based on memorization; integration of family awareness and family support programs; physician well-being programs; and, an emphasis on informed patients accepting some responsibility for their own care. The doctor's ability to diagnose and heal must start with the doctor.

## THE STRESSED PHYSICIAN

Beset by worldly demands, ever competent, today's physicians are expected to cope gracefully with each day's surprises. Unflinching, doctors work to heal their patients' wounds, paying little attention to their own. Ignoring the advice they readily give out, perhaps thinking that *stress* is just a buzzword that does not apply to doctors, physicians perform, no matter what.

Having endured the grueling stresses of medical school, today's doctors are nonetheless ill prepared to contend with the cumulative stresses of professional life. The AMA says that 10% of physicians terminate their practice prematurely for one or more stress-related causes. If doctors are to survive and thrive, then they must examine the sources, symptoms, and specifics for this pernicious syndrome—stress.

At the accelerated pace of the twenty-first century, few professions are immune to the stresses of long commutes, conflicting demands, and excessive paperwork. However, physicians are subject to additional noteworthy pressures: uncertainty in both diagnosis and treatment; dealing with emergencies; confronting incurable illness; the need to be calm, genial, and mistake-free; dealing openly with topics that are difficult for both patients and doctors; balancing clinical detachment with compassion; putting patients' needs ahead of all others; attempting to heal those who may not want to accept treatment; institutionalized intimacy; a rapidly changing professional infrastructure; and, of course, enormous economic pressures and the ever-present threat of malpractice suits.

Attempts to cope may themselves be displays of strain, including emotional distancing, depression, psychosomatic illness, or even self-destructive behavior. Such conduct will assure eventual failure. Only a deliberate and consistent system of coping with stress will allow doctors to heal themselves as they heal their patients.

In developing such a system, doctors must grant themselves a measure of the care they normally devote exclusively to patients. They must recognize that they too have needs, and must find satisfactory methods for meeting them. They must seek effective ways to cope with the stresses unique to medical practitioners, and they must acknowledge their own emotions and find comfortable ways of expressing them.

The needs of physicians are little different from those of patients. Doctors have physical requirements, such as nutrition, rest, exercise, and recreation. They need close, warm, supportive relationships. They must have self-definition, a sense of purpose, self-esteem, and security.

In tending to the needs of patients, doctors may shortchange themselves by eating poorly, resting inadequately, exercising impulsively, and deferring recreation altogether. They may substitute time spent with patients for nurturing relationships with families, friends, and peers. They may use a textbook description of their specialty in place of self-definition, purpose, and self-esteem, and they may allow rote behaviors to substitute for a true sense of security.

The first prescription in the defense against stress must be to attend to physical needs, and the greatest challenge here is time. A nutritious midday meal, a daily session on the treadmill, an occasional trip to the museum are simply appointments with yourself. Write them in your appointment book, take them seriously, and charge yourself for cancellations!

Next, seek supportive relationships. They too require time, but they also demand a measure of openness, which may fly in the face of the physician's professional demeanor. Unlike the one-way flow of support doctors provide to patients, friendships must allow a trusted exchange—both speaking and listening. Such support may grow out of slowly nurtured individual friendships or from professionally facilitated groups of colleagues or friends carefully selected to engender safety, privacy, and candor.

Self-definition is more than the facts on a curriculum vitae. It includes personality, motivation, goals, and spiritual qualities. If doctors examine the collective effect of these elements and identify those that are most important, they will begin to see the outlines of self-definition. Equally important, purpose grows out of a set of aspirations that are in harmony with that self-definition.

Doctors may easily confuse economic success or the admiration of patients or peers with self-esteem, but self-esteem must be derived from an internal sense of worthiness, competence, value, and confidence. Self-esteem relieves individuals from the pressing need to prove themselves to others and enables them to find reward within themselves.

Security, again, is easily confused with status. A sense of security grows from the integration of physical and mental health, self-definition, purpose, and self-esteem. In turn, it makes individuals more resilient to change and stress, more responsive to intellectual challenge, and more truly empathic to patients and peers.

Faced daily with matters of life and death, physicians may be demanding perfection from themselves where none is possible. If they consistently fail to measure up to this impossible yardstick, they may experience cumulative feelings of inadequacy, resentment, guilt, and humiliation, leading to overwork and chronic anxiety. Through personal discipline, counseling, or assertiveness training, today's doctors must learn to recognize and accept their human frailties and set limits on their performance. By marshalling their resources and accepting their limitations, they reduce their anxiety and vulnerability to stress.

The final battle in the war on stress is acknowledging and expressing emotions. Confronting pain, fear, anger, death, frustration, and confusion, doctors must often defer their own reactions in favor of their patients' needs. They may get in the habit of withdrawing, believing that they are protected from the messy turmoil of emotions. However, shielding themselves from the painful feelings also prevents them from experiencing the joys and satisfactions of their profession. They may displace or deny the expression of anger, subverting it into chronic resentment, blame, depression, or physical symptoms.

Learning to manage emotions productively requires patience, practice, and trust. Doctors must first recognize their own feelings and accept them as normal. They must then find ways to express them without harming themselves or others. And they must finally examine the freight of information that is carried in every emotional reaction. Anger may mean that some basic need was not met. Depression may mean that the individual has lost the hope of ever meeting that basic need. As doctors explore this information, test their reactions, and learn effective ways of expressing emotion, they give themselves a powerful inoculation against the destructive forces of stress.

In accepting their role as physicians, doctors are automatically accepting a measure of stress. They may well find it easier to number the things that are not stressful in their lives than those that are. There is nothing to indicate that this profession—or the world itself—is about to become stress-free. The solution lies in examining working conditions and habits, and making changes to assure that doctors are meeting their own needs, coping effectively with the inevitable stresses, and productively expressing their emotions. Doctors can only succeed in caring for patients if they successfully care for themselves. *Physician, heal thyself.*

## BURNOUT ASSESSMENT AND REDUCTION

In today's competitive world, few activities are immune to stress. From students and athletes to office and factory workers, from caregivers and volunteers to executives and physicians, every pursuit has its own level of demand, expectation, and personal cost. Because physicians and health professionals are subjected to a substantial burden of physical, economic, and emotional stress, they are particularly subject to burnout. The identification, assessment, and reduction of burnout are the first steps in more effective personal and practice management.

According to the Center for Professional Well-Being, "burnout is a stress syndrome, felt by sufferers as emotional exhaustion." Failure to treat burnout can lead to more serious symptoms and dysfunction. Among the symptoms and expressions of burnout are the following:

- *somatic,* including exhaustion, insomnia, G.I. disturbances, rapid breath;
- *emotional,* including sadness and depressed mood, negativism, decreased creativity, and increased cynicism; and,
- *interpersonal,* including quickness to anger, defensiveness, edginess and being ready to blame others, and a negative worldview.

Physicians experiencing burnout may feel "a lack of personal accomplishment" in their work and less commitment to their practice. They may decrease contact with patients and staff, listen less respectfully, be more irritable, order more tests, and, not surprisingly, provide care that is less satisfactory to their patients.

## Worst Case: Depression and Suicide

While the problems of depression and suicide among physicians have been observed and measured since the 1850s, medical training and culture has done little to acknowledge or reduce their occurrence. Although their mortality risks are otherwise lower, physicians have a higher rate of depression and suicide than the general population; the numbers are even higher among female physicians. However, according to a 2003 article in JAMA, "Low priority is given to physician mental health and physicians seeking help with these issues are often punished through discrimination in medical licensing, hospital privileges, and professional advancement." Such punitive responses only compound the problems of doctors already under immeasurable stress.

Personal, professional, and financial stressors correlate with depression and suicide—but, interestingly, not as direct causes. Instead, research shows that individuals with affective disorders experience stress more intensely. Worried about the costs, the stigma, or the loss of professional stature, doctors may simply forgo treatment and avoid discussing their concerns or symptoms with anyone. With ready access to drugs, the decision to self-medicate may be made without a second thought.

The evidence indicates that, in addition to direct treatment, physicians can benefit from some of the activities that they set aside because of the pressures on their time, such as social support and religious faith. American Foundation for Suicide Prevention experts recommend that physicians screen all patients for depression, thereby increasing their awareness of the condition's symptoms—in their patients, in their peers, and in themselves.

Because of the long-prevailing attitude discouraging discussion and management of physician depression and suicide, there have been few studies and little research on the subject. However, a shift is happening in professional attitudes to encourage physicians to seek help. Medical schools, associations, licensing boards, and hospitals are realizing the importance of physicians maintaining their balance and seeking care without professional repercussions. To take better care of patients, physicians must take better care of themselves.

## SPIRITUALITY

Some healing occurs without any logical or scientific basis. For many people, this is a result of strong spiritual beliefs and feelings. All physicians should learn to respect this in their patients. This is another instance of how we can learn important things from our patients. For many of us it is important that we become aware of our own spirituality, which gives us strength, insight, and hope. When patients perceive this in you, they are uplifted by your very presence.

# HEALING...AND STAYING HEALTHY

Not enough time. Too much pressure. Too many patients. Overwhelming financial and administrative obligations. These familiar attributes of the physician's life are just the tip of the iceberg when it comes to a serious affliction that can strike doctors at any stage of their career: compassion fatigue. Otherwise known as burnout, *compassion fatigue* can undermine physical and emotional health as well as personal and professional effectiveness.

As responsibilities increase and rewards decrease, doctors maintain extremely high expectations for their own performance. In an attempt to meet the ever-growing demands on their time, pressured physicians may sacrifice family time, exercise, regular meals, sleep, enriching conversations with colleagues and friends, and other types of recreation and relaxation. Instead of refueling physically and emotionally, they ignore their personal needs and end up *running on empty,* with nothing left for themselves—or their patients.

Compassion fatigue is every bit as debilitating as any other major illness—even for a skilled healer. As with other acute diseases, prompt treatment will yield the best results. Here are some suggestions for dealing with this pervasive condition:

- **Recognize the problem.** Are you feeling overwhelmed, exhausted, unsympathetic, annoyed, or hopeless? Have your sleeping, eating, or exercise habits changed? Do you tend to blame others when things go wrong? Are you trying to cram several activities into every precious moment? Any combination of these symptoms may indicate compassion fatigue.

- **Remember that you are not alone.** Although doctors may be reluctant to discuss it openly, compassion fatigue is common in today's multitasking world.

- **Take some time off.** By the time the problem is advanced enough to recognize, the solution is no longer a quick fix. Although time off seems impossible, you are doing yourself and your patients a disservice by continuing work once you have reached this point. You will need some time to retrain your system—to replace the get-along bad habits with productive, healthful behaviors.

- **Prescribe healthy activities.** If you were your own patient, what would you recommend? More exercise, more balanced and relaxed meals, increased time with family and friends, and having fun!

- **Talk with someone.** Seek a compassionate listener—a support group, counselor, clergy member, or colleague who can understand and help you gain perspective on the issues you are facing. The American Medical Association offers a variety of services that can help doctors deal with addiction, depression, and stress-related conditions.

- **Take time for yourself.** One of the most consistent symptoms of compassion fatigue is lack of personal time. Restoring health means carving out time for yourself: time to read, write letters, go to a movie, take a walk, or do absolutely nothing.

- **Postpone critical decisions.** If possible, put off big life changes for a while. When you are deep in the throes of compassion fatigue, the lure of a new job, new spouse, or new motorcycle may seem like the perfect balm. It is not.

- **Step back from complaining and blaming.** If you seem to be surrounded by incompetence, resist the temptation to cast blame on those around you. Consider the possibility that if your life were more balanced, you might be more accepting of others' humanness.

- **Set some limits.** Identify the elements of your life and your practice that are most rewarding and create a working/living plan that will allow you to reach those goals. Establish priorities and set limits on your time. Use these guidelines as you make decisions about new commitments and the direction of your life and career.

- **Once you have returned to work, watch for recurring symptoms.** Compassion fatigue crept up on you the first time and relapses can occur. If you find yourself taking refuge in drugs or alcohol or experiencing symptoms such as depression, anger, physical distress (headaches, hypertension, gastrointestinal problems) or reduced self-esteem, break the cycle again and pay more attention to your healthful habits.

Your choice of a career in medicine identifies you as a high-achieving, compassionate, hardworking individual. It is exactly these qualities that make you vulnerable to the undermining effects of compassion fatigue. Whether you are experiencing its very first symptoms or are already feeling that all is lost, it is not too late to regain your life and your career. Take action today—for the lasting benefit of yourself *and* your patients.

# chapter seventeen:
# A Perspective from Experience

There is no single way to start a medical practice. Each person is unique and each situation is unique. You may learn from others' experiences how to avoid some of the pitfalls that are likely to occur in the early life of your practice, but undoubtedly you will have stories of your own to pass along to younger practitioners when you are ready to retire.

The lifeblood of the medical practice is patients. Treat them well and you will do well. Answer their phone calls, or if you really cannot, designate someone in your practice to do so. Access to you is vital to your patients' well-being.

Your team, working together, can make all of you a smashing success. Treat them as valued teammates, with respect and a healthy measure of good humor. You cannot change yourself into something that you are not. Do what you do naturally and be on constant guard to correct bad habits. Short tempers, indifference, and lack of respect can be changed.

You are going to be practicing medicine for a long, long time. Your reputation will last a long time as well. It will gain momentum the longer you practice, and you should do nothing to cast a negative light on your reputation as a fine, successful doctor.

Cultivate your reputation in the medical community. It will pay off many times over as you deal with other doctors. Civility reduces hostility, and reduced hostility lowers stress, making difficult situations more tolerable. Remember the building blocks for establishing a successful medical practice:

- communication with patients;
- commitment to patients' care;
- competence in such care; and,
- conscientious billing.

These four "Cs" will remind you of the important and yet simple actions that you have to take to build a medical practice.

## CLOSING COMMENTS

A medical practice is an organization with its own personality, its own culture, and its own future. Your staff wants to make it successful, because if it is, the staff will prosper. If they feel that they are contributing to that success and sharing it through meaningful work, bonuses, raises, or profit-sharing, they will be motivated to do the best that they can to provide quality patient care and help the practice succeed.

People are also motivated by effective communication. Praise and positive comments are as valuable as raises and bonuses to motivate people. Make no mistake, the personality of a company starts at the top, right from the beginning. You set the tone. If you blame others, take all the credit, do not communicate, and fail to meet your commitments, you will soon find yourself surrounded by people who reflect that style. If you are honest, direct, competent, and willing to admit and resolve your mistakes, you will attract other doctors, staff, and patients with the same qualities. You may have super-human expectations of yourself, but you will be sharing your office and your professional life with people who are *just human*. If you honor their humanity, you might find that some of it rubs off on you.

You need to define and develop the culture of your practice from the outset. It is vital for a working team to have a feeling of camaraderie and identity. Attitudes, traditions, and rules are all part of that culture.

Office traditions help to cement working teams. Something as simple as having lunch together on Fridays can reward your staff for their hard work. The celebration of important dates, such as the anniversary of the founding of the practice, birthdays, and holidays can contribute to a shared culture.

There are many ways of showing appreciation. For one of your employees, an extra hour at lunch or a gift certificate at a local restaurant may be more meaningful than a bouquet of flowers. Learn what would be most valued by your staff. Year-end bonuses and profit-sharing are also part of the practice culture, and those are options that should be seriously considered, even though you may not yet have any permanent employees. An infant practice is like any other infant—it will grow and mature with positive nurturing.

Consistent and predictable management will help your medical practice succeed. The people—you, in this case—who oversee the organization and its activities must ensure that ground rules are established and followed. That way, everyone knows what is expected of them, and anyone who is working against the rules can be easily identified and appropriate action can be taken. These rules act as much to provide a model as they do to create consistent behavior throughout the practice. They apply to everyone. The boss is not exempt.

It is the obligation of the founder of the practice to set an example to communicate to the staff, the other doctors, and the public the vision that the founder has in mind for the practice. A culture of honesty, hard work, clear communication, and mutual respect will assure that your practice has rewarding work, happy staff, and satisfied patients for many years to come.

It is our hope that you have a very successful business and a fulfilling professional medical practice, that you care for yourself as well as you would a patient, and that you maintain your passion for medicine and healing throughout your career and your lifetime.

# appendix:
# Resources

Nearly every state, hospital, professional or specialty association, university, and medical school offers online resources for physicians that can be extremely useful. In addition, following are some valuable resources that can extend your practice's library of printed materials. (Although most of these sites have a long and established presence on the Internet, Web addresses do change. However, all sites were operational at press time.)

## ONLINE RESOURCES

**American Academy of Family Physicians**
**www.aafp.org**
Extensive resources on practice management, clinical care and research, policy and advocacy, careers, and other topics.

**American Association for the Advancement of Science**
**www.aaas.org**
An international nonprofit organization dedicated to advancing science around the world by serving as an educator, leader, spokesperson, and professional association. Publisher of the journal *Science*.

## American College of Physicians
**www.acponline.org**
The nation's largest medical specialty society, with about 119,000 members, publishes journals and books, and offers a variety of valuable online resources.

## American Medical Association
**www.ama-assn.org**
Extensive resources on every aspect of medical practice. In addition to the rich selection of materials accessible from the main site, the AMA also provides sites focused on the needs and concerns of particular subgroups of physicians, including the following.

GLBT Advisory Committee:
**www.ama-assn.org/ama/pub/category/14753.html**

Group and Faculty Practice Physicians:
**www.ama-assn.org/ ama/pub/category/1736.html**

International Medical Graduates:
**www.ama-assn.org/ama/pub/category/17.html**

Medical Students' Section:
**www.ama-assn.org/ama/pub/category/14.html**

Minority Affairs Consortium:
**www.ama-assn.org/ama/pub/category/20.html**

Organized Medical Staff Section:
**www.ama-assn.org/ama/pub/category/21.html**

Resident and Fellow Section:
**www.ama-assn.org/ama/pub/category/15.html**

Section on Medical Schools:
**www.ama-assn.org/ama/pub/category/1843.html**

Senior Physicians Group:
**www.ama-assn.org/ama/pub/category/23.html**

Women Physicians Congress:
**www.ama-assn.org/ama/pub/category/18.html**

Young Physicians Section:
**www.ama-assn.org/ama/pub/category/16.html**

## American Nurses Association
**www.nursingworld.org**
News, initiatives, career information, standards and ethics, and much more.

## Centers for Medicare and Medicaid Services
**www.cms.hhs.gov**
Up-to-date information about Medicare and Medicaid.

## Centers for Disease Control and Prevention
**www.cdc.gov**
Up-to-date information about infectious and chronic diseases, injuries, workplace hazards, disabilities, and environmental health threats, as well as valuable travelers' health advisories and immunization information.

## Certification Commission for Healthcare Information Technology
**www.cchit.org**
A voluntary, private-sector initiative to certify healthcare information technology (HIT) products in order to open up the flow of HIT incentives, reduce the risk for HIT purchasers, and act as a catalyst to HIT adoption.

## Department of Health and Human Services
**www.dhhs.gov**
Up-to-date information on a variety of health conditions and factors.

## The Doctors Page
**www.doctorspage.net/satisf.asp**
A variety of useful resources and links for practicing physicians.

## Doctors Without Borders
**www.doctorswithoutborders.org**
Information about this international, independent medical humanitarian organization that delivers emergency aid to people affected by armed conflict, epidemics, natural and man-made disasters, and exclusion from health care.

## EurekAlert!
**www.eurekalert.org/bysubject/medicine.php**
An online, global news service operated by AAAS with links to full-text current articles on medical issues from a wide variety of sources.

## Electronic Health Record (EHR) Information and Selection
**www.aafp.org/fpm/20050200/55howt.html**
Adler, Kenneth G., "How to Select an Electronic Health Record System."

## Centers for Medicare and Medicaid Services
**www.cms.hhs.gov/PhysicianFocusedQualInits**
Describes the HHS involvement in the promotion of effective information technology.

## Healthcare Information and Management Systems Society
**www.himss.org**
A membership organization focused on providing leadership for the optimal use of health care information technology and management systems.

**Health Level Seven**
**www.hl7.org**
Extensive information about the HL7 protocol, which creates standards for the exchange, management, and integration of electronic healthcare information.

**HIPAA information and resources**
**www.hipaa.org**
Everything you ever wanted to know about the Health Insurance Portability and Accountability Act of 1996.

**CALHIPAA information and resources**
**www.calhipaa.com**
CAL HIPAA is the largest HIPAA educational resource for individual health care providers and group practices nationwide.

**Hospice Foundation of America**
**www.hospicefoundation.org**
Includes national and regional programs and information for those who cope either personally or professionally with terminal illness, death, and the process of grief.

**Joint Commission on Accreditation of**
**Healthcare Organizations**
**www.jcaho.org**
Provides health care accreditation and related services that support performance improvement in health care organizations.

**Journal of the American Medical Association**
**http://jama.ama-assn.org**
Current and archived issues of JAMA.

**Medical Strategic Planning, Inc.**
**www.medsp.com**
Provides information on EHR, medical life support, and computer practice management.

## Medicare
**www.medicare.gov**

The official Medicare website, with everything you and your patients need to know about Medicare and the Medicare Modernization Act.

## MedLaw
**www.medlaw.com**

Health law resources for healthcare professionals, hospitals, and their attorneys.

## MomMD
**www.mommd.com**

An association and online magazine for allopathic and osteopathic women in medicine.

## National Center for Biotechnology Information
**www.ncbi.nlm.nih.gov**

Creates public databases, conducts research in computational biology, develops software tools for analyzing genome data, and disseminates biomedical information for the better understanding of molecular processes affecting human health and disease.

## National Coalition for Health Professional Education in Genetics
**www.nchpeg.org**

Promotes health professional education and access to information about advances in human genetics.

## National Human Genome Research Institute
**www.genome.gov**

Information for health professionals and the public on resources and technology for genome research and its application to human health.

## National Institutes of Health
**www.nih.gov**

Valuable information on NIH-supported programs designed to improve health by conducting and supporting research into the causes, diagnosis, prevention, and cure of human diseases, disorders, etc.

## National Institute of Mental Health
**www.nimh.nih.gov**

Breaking news, mental health information, research and funding, and much more.

## National Library of Medicine
**www.nlm.nih.gov**

The world's largest medical library; collects materials and provides information and research services in all areas of biomedicine and health care. Includes a searchable medical dictionary.

## Occupational Safety and Health Administration
**www.osha.gov**

Nearly 450,000 pages of information, including a special section devoted to assisting small businesses.

## PubMed
**www.pubmed.gov**

PubMed is a service of the National Library of Medicine that includes over fifteen million citations from MEDLINE and other life science journals dating back to the 1950s. Includes links to full-text articles and other related resources.

# RISK MANAGEMENT

**Cooperative of American Physicians, Inc.,**
**Mutual Protection Trust (CAP-MPT)**
**www.cap-mpt.com**
Risk Management Self-Assessment Kit, 2004

**http://info.med.yale.edu/caim/risk/contents.html**
Issues in Risk Management from Yale-New Haven Hospital and
Yale University School of Medicine

**SCORE**
**www.score.org**
SCORE is a national nonprofit organization and a resource
partner with the U.S. Small Business Administration. Through its
online services and local volunteer network, SCORE provides
confidential business counseling and training.

**Society of Hospital Medicine (SHM)**
**www.hospitalmedicine.org**
Established to support the work of hospitalists. Website provides
details on the practice of hospital medicine.

*Wall Street Journal* **Center for Entrepreneurs**
**www.startupjournal.com**
Offers a variety of resources for new businesses, principally
drawn from the *Wall Street Journal.*

# BOOKS ON THE BUSINESS OF MEDICINE

**NOTE:** *Some books may also be available as audiotapes or CDs.*
*Check your medical library, bookstore, or online resource.*

*Assessing the Value of the Medical Practice*, Second Edition,
John P. Reiboldt, The Coker Group, AMA Press, 2004.

*The Business of Medical Practice – Advanced Profit Maximization Techniques for Savvy Doctors,* 2nd Edition, Edited by David Edward Marcinko, Editor, Springer Publishing Company, 2004.

*Dealing with Difficult People – How to Deal with Nasty Customers, Demanding Bosses and Annoying Co-workers,* Roberta Cava, Firefly Books, 1999, 2004.

*The E Myth Revisited – Why Most Small Businesses Don't Work and What to Do About It,* Michael E. Gerber, Harper Collins Publishers, 1995.

*Essentials of Medical Management,* Edited by Wesley Curry and Barbara J. Linney, MA, American Colleges of Physician Executives, 2003.

*Executive Thinking – The Dream, The Vision, The Mission Achieved,* Leslie Kossoff, Davis-Black Publishing, 1999.

*Financial Management of the Medical Practice,* J. Max Reibolt, American Medical Association, 2002.

 *Going Into Medical Practice,* Rebecca B. Campen, Blackwell Publishers, 2002.

*Handbook of Medical Office Communications, Effective Letters, Memos, and Emails,* The Coker Group, AMA Press, 2005.

*Healing the Wounds: A Physician Looks at his Work,* David Hilfiker, Pantheon Books, 1985.

*The Health Care Provider's Guide to Facing the Malpractice Deposition,* Constance G. Uribe, M.D., F.A.C.S. CRC Press LLC, 2000.

*HIPAA Plain and Simple, A Compliance Guide for Health Care Professionals,* Carolyn P. Hartley, MLA, CHP and Edward D. Jones, III, AMA Press, 2004.

*How To Excel During Depositions: Techniques for Experts That Work*, Steven Babitsky, Esq., and James J. Mangraviti, Jr., Esq., S-E-A-K, Inc. Legal and Medical Information Systems, 1999.

*Human Error*, James Reason, Cambridge University Press, 1990.

*The Jurisprudent Physician – A Physician's Guide to Legal Process and Malpractice Litigation*, Margaret Dean, BSN., J.D., 1999.

*Managing the Medical Practice*, Second Edition, Crystal S. Reeves, The Coker Group, AMA Press, 2003.

*Marketing the Physician Practice*, Stanley R. Joseph, AMA Press, 2000.

*Personnel Management in the Medical Practice*, Second Edition, Kay B. Stanley, The Coker Group, AMA Press, 2002.

*Physician Practice Management – Essential Operational and Financial Knowledge*, Lawrence F. Wolper, FACMPE, Jones and Bartlett Publishers, 2005.

*A Physician's Guide – Adverse Events, Stress and Litigation*, Sara C. Charles, M.D. and Paul R. Frisch, J.D., Oxford University Press, 2005.

*A Physician's Self-Paced Guide to Critical Thinking*, Milos Jenicek, AMA Press, 2006.

*Practice Management: A Practical Guide to Starting and Running a Medical Office*, Christian Rainer, Wyndham Hall Press, 2004.

*The Resilient Physician – Effective Emotional Management for Doctors and Their Medical Organizations*, Wayne M. Sotile and Mary O. Sotile, American Medical Association, 2002.

*The Resilient Practitioner – Burnout Prevention and Self-Care Strategies for Counselors, Therapists, Teachers, and Health Professionals,* Thomas M. Skovholt, Allyn & Bacon, 2001.

*Starting a Medical Practice,* Jeffrey P. Daigrepont, American Medical Association, 2nd Edition, 2003.

*Twelve Months to Your Ideal Private Practice: A Workbook,* Lynn Grodzki, W. W. Norton & Co., 2003.

*The Yale Management Guide for Physicians,* Stephen Rimar, Wiley, 2001.

# PERSONAL GROWTH BOOKS

*The Art of JAMA: One Hundred Covers and Essays From The Journal of the American Medical Association,* M. Therese Southgate, M.D., AMA Press, 1997.

*The Art of JAMA II: Covers and Essays From The Journal of the American Medical Association,* M. Therese Southgate, M.D., AMA Press, 2001.

*Body for Life: 12 Weeks to Mental and Spiritual Strength,* Bill Phillips, Harper Collins, 1999.

*8 Minutes in the Morning,* Jorge Cruise, Harper Collins, 2001.

*E-Myth Master: The Seven Essential Disciplines for Building a World Class Company,* Michael Gerber, Harper Business, 2004.

*The Four Agreements: A Practical Guide to Personal Freedom,* Don Miguel Ruiz, Amber-Allen, 1999.

*The Game of Work: How to Enjoy Work as Much as Play,* Charles A Coonradt, Game of Work Publishing, 1997.

*Healers on Healing*, Edited by Richard Carlson, Ph.D., and Benjamin Shield, Larcher Publishing, Inc., 1989.

*How to Get your Point Across in 30 Seconds or Less*, Milo O. Frank, Pocket Book, 1986.

*The Medical Marriage, Sustaining Healthy Relationships for Physicians and Their Families*, Wayne M. Sotile, Ph.D., and Mary O. Sotile, M.A., AMA Press, 2000.

*A Piece of My Mind*, Edited by Roxanne K. Young, A New Collection of Essays From JAMA The Journal of the American Medical Association, AMA Press, 2000.

*The Power of Now: A Guide to Spiritual Enlightenment*, Eckhart Tolle, New World, 1999.

*The Power of the Pitch/Transform Yourself Into A Persuasive Presenter and Win More Business*, Gary Hawkins, Dearborn, 2005.

*The Procrastinator's Handbook: Mastering the Art of Doing It Now*, Rita Emmet, Walker Publishing, 2000.

*The Sedona Method: Your Key to Lasting Happiness, Success, Peace and Emotional Wellbeing*, Hale Dwoskin, Sedona, Arizona, Sedona Press, 2003.

*The Seven Spiritual Laws of Success*, Deepak Chopra, Amber-Allen, 1994.

*The Soul of the Physician: Doctors Speaking About Passion, Resilience, and Hope*, Linda Gambee Henry, James Douglas Henry, AMA Press, 2002.

*Start Small, Finish Big: Fifteen Key Lessons to Start and Run Your Own Successful Business*, Fred DeLuca with John B. Hayes, Warner Books, 2000.

*Stress Management Made Simple*, Jay Winner, M.D., Flue Fountain Press, 2003.

*The Successful Principles: How to Get from Where You Are to Where you Want to Be*, Jack Canfield, Harper Collins, 2005.

*Think and Grow Rich*, Napoleon Hill, Fawcett Crest, 1960.

*The Way of the Spiritual Warrior* (audio cassette), with David Gershon. Available from Rio Web - www.empowermenttraining.com.

*The Wealthy Spirit: Daily Affirmations for Financial Stress Reduction*, Chellie Campbell, Sourcebooks, 2002.

# Index

## A

accountants, 5, 30, 56, 67, 71, 79, 80, 82, 83, 95, 96, 118, 130

administration, 11, 23, 69, 81, 94, 104, 112, 113, 117, 124

advance directives, 53, 164, 165

advanced practice nurses, 71

advertising, 12, 87, 149, 150

after-hours phone calls, 28, 204

alternative dispute resolution (ADR), 184, 188, 189

American College of Medical Practice Executives (ACMPE), 112

American Medical Association, 38, 86, 91, 100, 132, 137, 149, 158, 160, 162, 208, 218, 220, 228

Americans with Disabilities Act, 66

anger, 174, 191, 196, 197, 223, 225, 229

anxiety, 35, 93, 101, 200, 223

apologies, 192, 195, 196, 197

appointments, 13, 14, 35, 45, 48, 54, 76, 103, 105, 110, 124, 143, 146, 156, 157, 195, 198, 199, 204, 209, 222

arbitration, 125, 139, 184, 187, 188, 189, 190

arrogance, 136, 191

assets, 11, 20, 24, 93, 94, 171, 184

attorneys, 7, 25, 124, 165, 167, 169, 171, 172, 173, 176, 178, 179, 180, 181, 182, 188

## B

bank accounts, 29

banks, 82, 83, 84, 94

benefits, 12, 17, 20, 21, 22, 23-24, 58, 62, 66, 67, 79, 81,

86, 88, 117, 122, 123, 137, 162, 171, 186, 226, 229
billing, 14, 18, 54, 55, 56, 63, 82, 101, 116, 118, 121, 122, 123, 124, 125, 127, 128, 129, 204, 232
bookkeepers, 5, 18, 71, 72, 95
budgets, 1, 6, 10, 12, 33, 48, 54, 56, 61, 100, 101, 145, 153
building a base, 147
burnout, 220, 224, 225, 227
business managers, 81
business plan, 9, 10, 11, 12, 27, 60, 81, 145

## C

capital, 19, 31, 41, 42, 58, 69, 90, 93, 95
cash flow, 5, 9, 11, 31, 83, 101, 102
chart, 103, 105, 114, 116, 117, 122, 124, 141, 142, 158, 164, 203, 207, 208
Civil Rights Act of 1964, 65, 134
colleagues, 42, 50, 62, 67, 68, 69, 86, 113, 132, 152, 218, 222, 227
collections, 39, 43, 116, 121, 122, 123, 124, 125, 126, 127, 128, 129, 130, 204

commitment, 61, 80, 198, 225, 232
communication, 29, 37, 40, 47, 55, 60, 62, 66, 105, 113, 127, 129, 149, 152, 157, 184, 198, 199, 200, 206, 209, 213, 232, 234
community, 2, 3, 4, 135, 136, 146, 147, 148, 150, 151, 152, 167, 170, 218, 232
compassion fatigue, 227, 228, 229
competence, 147, 153, 170, 171, 222, 232
competition, 5, 10, 11, 12, 61
computers, 37, 43, 50, 52, 55, 60, 145
    hardware, 28, 50, 51, 52, 54, 57
    medical practice management (MPM) software, 55
    software, 10, 11, 28, 50, 51, 53, 54, 55, 56, 57, 58, 61, 63, 74, 106
concierge medicine, 13
confidentiality, 33, 36, 76, 140, 202, 204
conflicts of interest, 80, 139
consultants, 15, 42, 50, 71, 73, 77, 79, 80, 192, 205
consultation, 157, 214, 215
continuing care, 156, 157
corporations, 10, 15, 20, 21, 22, 23, 24, 25, 26, 29

cost recovery, 213

courts, 88, 137, 176, 184, 189

credentials, 80, 115, 151, 166

credit, 9, 11, 29, 32, 41, 83, 84, 94, 95, 121, 122, 129, 150, 232

Current Procedural Terminology (CPT), 56, 124

customer service, 122

## D

deadbeats, 125

debt, 83, 95, 96, 100, 139

defendant, 165, 172, 173, 174, 178, 180, 181

defensive medicine, 208

delinquent accounts, 126

depositions, 166, 173, 174, 175, 178

depression, 93, 191, 220, 221, 223, 224, 225, 226, 228, 229

disability, 17, 22, 86, 87, 88, 133

discipline reports, 133

disclosures, 161

discounts, 41, 90, 149

discrimination, 66, 133, 225

doing business as (DBA), 28

drugs, 131, 162, 163, 218, 226, 229

## E

Electronic Health Records (EHR), 28, 51, 52, 53, 55, 56, 57, 58, 59, 60, 61, 62, 82, 117

emergency, 29, 44, 77, 85, 105, 124, 128, 156, 163, 207, 211

Employee Retirement Income Security Act, 67

employees, 16, 18, 22, 24, 37, 50, 65, 66, 67, 69, 72, 75, 77, 82, 84, 85, 87, 117, 118, 123, 134, 233

employer identification number (EIN), 30

employment agency, 68

employment agreements, 23, 115

equipment, 11, 33, 37, 41, 42, 43, 44, 45, 47, 49, 50, 51, 52, 53, 55, 57, 58, 59, 60, 61, 63, 77, 83, 94, 101, 103, 115, 145, 202, 203, 207

ethics, 131, 132, 133, 136, 137, 138, 139

executive summary, 11

## F

Federal Family Education Loan (FFEL), 98

fee disputes, 139, 212

fee structure, 121

fidelity bond, 87

filing systems, 38, 43, 69, 77,
    104, 129, 204
finances, 1, 31, 41, 81, 125, 196
firm agreements, 25
follow up, 13, 14, 103, 156,
    193, 199, 204, 206, 207, 214
forbearance, 98
furnishings, 31, 83

# G

giving lectures, 148
goals, 11, 12, 16, 60, 75, 80,
    81, 100, 153, 217, 222, 229
Good Samaritan laws, 136, 156
guarantee of results, 163

# H

Health Care Financing Admin-
    istration (HCFA), 124
Health Insurance Portability
    and Accountability Act
    (HIPAA), 61, 140, 156, 161,
    162, 164
hearing, 166, 176, 178, 183
hospitalists, 13, 14, 15
hospitals, 2, 3, 4, 6, 14, 15, 42,
    47, 58, 68, 70, 77, 86, 89,
    90, 91, 114, 115, 116, 135,
    148, 151, 160, 161, 187, 188,
    189, 190, 194, 197, 207, 225,
    226

human resources (HR), 73, 76,
    112, 117, 118

# I

income, 12, 16, 17, 20, 21, 22,
    25, 27, 67, 79, 82, 93, 94,
    95, 96, 97, 98, 101, 118, 145
indexing, 53, 77, 103
informed consent, 131, 156,
    162, 163, 164, 193, 214
injury, 24, 88, 114, 139, 159,
    166, 167, 175
insurance, 5, 11, 12, 15, 20, 22,
    24, 30, 56, 62, 67, 73, 77,
    79, 82, 83, 84, 85, 86, 87,
    88, 105, 114, 115, 116, 117,
    122, 123, 124, 125, 126, 129,
    143, 146, 161, 171, 172, 173,
    187, 189, 200, 204, 205, 206
    claims-made, 85
    occurrence, 85, 225
    tail coverage, 85
intensivists, 13, 14
interest rate, 97, 98, 99
interview, 28, 50, 71, 74, 75,
    134

# J

Joint Commission on Accredi-
    tation of Healthcare Organi-
    zations (JCAHO), 193

jurisdictions, 20, 25, 85, 132,
    133, 135, 136, 138, 139, 141,
    158, 159, 167, 171, 173, 176,
    178, 179, 180, 183, 187
jury, 167, 169, 173, 174, 176,
    179, 180, 181, 187

# L

laboratories, 3, 4, 13, 14, 44,
    60, 70, 103, 115, 116, 172,
    203, 204, 206, 208
lawsuits, 85, 138, 159, 160, 165,
    169, 171, 173, 175, 178, 186,
    190, 191, 192, 198, 200, 205,
    212
lawyer. *See attorneys*
lease, 6, 7, 28, 31, 41, 42, 43,
    83, 145
liability, 11, 15, 16, 20, 23, 24,
    25, 85, 86, 87, 88, 114, 136,
    156, 162, 165, 169, 170, 171,
    174, 175, 176, 178, 188, 192,
    193, 200
licenses, 9, 12, 27, 70, 115,
    133, 135
limited liability company (LLC),
    25
limited liability partnership
    (LLP), 19, 20
litigation, 170, 172, 173, 184-
    185, 187, 197
loans, 9, 11, 12, 82, 84, 95, 96,
    97, 98, 99, 100, 102

location, 1, 2, 3, 5, 6, 7, 11, 17,
    31, 67, 77, 90, 107, 116, 217
    medium-sized city, 2, 3, 4
    metropolitan area, 2, 4, 5
    small town, 2, 3, 4, 146

# M

maintenance, 7, 18, 35, 39, 57,
    61, 63, 70, 115, 116, 202,
    204
malpractice, 20, 85, 86, 133,
    136, 138, 142, 165, 167, 171,
    172, 175, 176, 178, 186, 191,
    192, 193, 194, 195, 196, 197,
    198, 199, 200, 201, 203, 205,
    206, 207, 209, 211, 213, 215,
    218, 221
management, 12, 17, 18, 19,
    22, 24, 38, 42, 55, 59, 60,
    63, 69, 72, 73, 80, 83, 86,
    91, 95, 96, 103, 106, 112,
    113, 114, 115, 118, 119, 192,
    199, 200, 201, 202, 205, 206,
    211, 214, 217, 224, 226, 233
mandatory continuing medical
    education, 171
marketing, 10, 11, 12, 113, 145,
    146, 147, 149, 150, 151, 152,
    153, 169
mediation, 26, 116, 139, 179,
    184, 185, 186, 187, 188, 189,
    190
Medicaid, 115

medical board, 137, 149, 212, 213, 215
medical book publisher, 90
Medical Injury Compensation Reform Act (MICRA), 88
medical library, 89
electronic, 91
Medicare, 83, 115
mistakes, 194, 195, 205, 213, 220, 232
moral turpitude, 137

## N

negotiation, 6, 7, 18, 116, 141, 184, 185, 188, 189, 190
networking, 3, 4, 50, 53, 86, 121, 147, 152
nurse practitioners, 68, 69, 70, 71, 72, 132, 134, 135
nurses, 36, 68, 69, 72, 132, 134

## O

Occupational Safety and Health Act, 66
office manager, 36, 42, 45, 60, 68, 72, 73, 74, 112, 145
office space, 5, 6, 18, 65, 69, 79, 89, 123, 145
on-call coverage, 28, 47, 204, 214

## P

parking, 2, 6, 7, 18, 28
partnerships, 15, 17, 19, 20, 21, 22, 24, 25, 26, 29, 69
agreements, 19
pass-throughs, 7, 25
patient flow, 113
pension, 20, 21, 23
photocopiers, 42, 77
physician impairment, 218, 220
physician/patient relationship, 109, 131, 140, 142, 143, 156, 159
privilege, 109, 136, 158, 159
Physicians Insurers Association of America (PIAA), 86
physicians' assistants, 68, 132, 134, 135
plaintiff, 159, 172, 173, 175, 178, 180, 181, 186, 190
policies and procedures, 75
press releases, 150, 151
privacy, 27, 33, 125, 140, 156, 160, 161, 203, 209, 222
profit-sharing, 19, 21, 77, 232, 233
public health, 59

## R

reception area, 31, 33, 35, 199
recordkeeping, 55, 58, 59, 124, 203, 207

references, 57, 68, 71, 74, 80,
    128, 134
rent, 3, 5, 7, 17, 28, 38, 41, 101
research, 14, 15, 30, 54, 55, 59,
    86, 89, 91, 104, 113, 225,
    226
résumés, 12, 71, 133
retainer, 13, 14, 23, 80
retirement, 17, 20, 21, 22, 66,
    67, 81
right of first refusal, 7
risk management, 114, 192,
    200, 201, 202, 205


S

safety, 59, 65, 66, 77, 105, 152,
    203, 204, 218, 222
salaries, 3, 12, 23, 123
security, 2, 7, 50, 53, 54, 56,
    59, 61, 62, 67, 83, 123, 161,
    217, 221, 222, 223
self-esteem, 221, 222, 223, 229
settlement, 174, 175, 179, 182,
    187, 188
sexual harassment, 87, 137,
    138
shareholders, 22, 25, 26, 94
skip patients, 128
Small Business Administration,
    11, 94
Social Security, 83, 123, 161
sole practitioner, 15, 16, 17, 23,
    94, 192

specialization, 2, 3, 4, 5, 9, 15,
    16, 30, 42, 60, 69, 70, 89,
    92, 121, 151, 167, 171, 178,
    182, 205, 214, 222
spirituality, 226
startup costs, 101
statute of limitations, 175
stress, 101, 114, 123, 125, 163,
    191, 200, 206, 217, 220, 221,
    222, 223, 224, 225, 228, 232
subpoena, 159, 166
suicide, 220, 225, 226
superbill, 124
surgeries, 5, 121
symptoms, 107, 124, 220, 223,
    224, 225, 226, 227, 228, 229


T

taxes, 7, 12, 20, 21, 22, 23, 25,
    27, 30, 31, 41, 43, 56, 72,
    81, 82, 83, 90, 117, 139
teaching, 3, 14, 15, 54, 70, 189
Telephone Intake Form, 47, 48
telephone system, 28, 43, 47
terminal illness, 166
terminating a patient, 85, 140,
    157
testimony, 138, 165, 166, 167,
    169, 173, 174, 175, 178, 180,
    188
treatments, 4, 5, 22, 26, 60, 73,
    91, 105, 106, 109, 111, 116,
    121, 124, 127, 134, 139, 140,

141, 142, 143, 151, 156,
158, 159, 160, 161, 162,
163, 165, 170, 188, 189,
192, 193, 194, 198, 203,
205, 206, 207, 214, 219,
221, 226, 227
trial, 165, 174, 175, 176, 178,
179, 180, 181, 182, 187

## U

uninterrupted power supply
(UPS), 54

## W

waiting room, 32, 33, 35, 39,
40, 194
website, 11, 48, 87, 146, 150,
151
witness, 156, 165, 166, 167,
169, 173, 174
expert, 165, 167, 169
workers' compensation, 67, 85,
88

## X

X-rays, 70, 116, 121, 172, 206,
208

# About the Authors

**Judge William Huss** is a full-time mediator and arbitrator, overseeing individual, institutional, and corporate cases. *Verdict Magazine* named him a Master Mediator. Judge Huss was on the Los Angeles Superior Court, presiding over both civil and criminal trials. He also served on the Los Angeles Superior Court Executive Committee and was the Chair of the Education Subcommittee.

He is cofounder of an alternative dispute resolution company and served as its president from 1996 to 2001. He has successfully conducted over 2,800 mediations on the subjects of construction, business, employment, insurance, bad faith, personal injury, eminent domain, malpractice, real estate, homeowners association, and many others.

Judge Huss received his JD degree from the University of Southern California School of Law. As a captain in the United States Naval Reserve Judge Advocate General Corps, he specialized in the law of war. He founded a law firm in downtown Los Angeles, and he is now of counsel to the firm. Having been an associate and partner in small, medium, and large firms, as well as founding one himself, Judge Huss is well qualified to share insights and experiences that will benefit professionals who want to start a firm themselves.

Judge Huss is a coauthor with Marlene Coleman, M.D. of *Home-owners Association and You; The Ultimate Guide to Harmonious Community Living* and the author of *Start Your Own Law Practice*, and the audiotape, "Winning Ways in Court."

**Dr. Marlene Coleman** is a board-certified Pediatrician practicing in Newport Beach, California for over twenty-five years. Her sub-specialty is in travel and adolescent medicine. She was honored as one of the Top Pediatricians in American for 2004–2005.

Dr. Coleman received her MD degree from the University of California at Irvis School of Medicine and is an Associate Clinical Professor of Family Medicine at the Keck School of Medicine at the University of Southern California (USC), where for over fifteen years she taught freshman medical students "Introduction to Clinical Medicine" and produced the audio tape, "Enjoying Your Practice of Medicine." She is also an attending physician at the California Institute of Technology (CalTech), employing her skills toward keeping students healthy as they study, lecture, and travel all over the world.

She serves on the Board of Trustees and Quality Review Board for the Cooperative of American Physicians/Mutual Protection Trust, a medical malpractice cooperative. As a Captain in the U.S. Naval Reserve Medical Corps, Dr. Coleman served in Washington, D.C., at the Navy Annex to the Pentagon.

She is the author of many articles and two books, *Safe and Sound, Healthy Travel with Children*, and a coauthor with Judge William Huss of *Homeowners Associations and You; The Ultimate Guide to Harmonious Community Living*.

Dr. Coleman's broad experience in medicine and medical liability management enables her to give a great deal of insight to those starting their practice.